'How to make a pleated skirt' is one of a series of books by DIYcouture.

Other titles in the series include:
How to make a cloak
How to make a wrap top
How to make a grecian dress
How to make a jump suit
How to make a gathered dress
How to make a straight skirt
How to make a kaftan
How to make a pair of trousers
How to make a tulip skirt
How to make a shrug
How to make a hoody

www.diy-couture.co.uk

Written by Rosie Martin
Construction illustrations and photography by Rosie Martin
Fashion photography by Gina Amama and Luka Yang
Cover image by Gina Amama: www.ginaamama.com
Clothing modelled by Jasiek Luka, Hannah Martin, Angela Hooker, Louise Rondel, Ethesham Haque, Danielle Doobay, Samantha Carrington, Laura Chapman, Stella Joseph and Miriam Newman
Design and typography by Rodger Martin and Rosie Martin
Edited by Angela Hooker, Mari Martin, Ann Shirley, Jessica Bevan, Kerrie Curzon, Craig Jordan-Baker and Toby Cullen
Artwork by Antuong Nguyen: antuong01@gmail.com

Published in the UK by Street Stroke Hothouse Press
10 Roding Road, London E5 0DW
© DIYcouture
Printed in the UK by Apple Colour
Silverthorne Lane, St. Philips, Bristol BS2 0QD

ISBN: 978-1-907520-00-6

How to make a pleated skirt

An instruction book by

Index

- (02) *DIYcouture* – where it has come from and what it aims to do
- (04) *You will need* – the tools you must have before you start making clothes
- (06) *Fabric* – choosing material and the effect your choice has on your garment
- (08) *The pleated skirt* – the pieces that make up the basic skirt
- (09) *Variations* – using this set of instructions to create a variety of styles
- (12) *Cutting your pieces*
- (14) *Zig-zag stitch*
- (16) *Making pleats*
- (20) *Straight stitch*
- (22) *Joining the front and back of your skirt*
- (28) *Making a waistband*
- (36) *Putting in a zip*
- (40) *Finishing the bottom edge*
- (44) *Joining multiple pieces of fabric*
- (47) *Silky Babies* – a series of illustrations by Antuong Nguyen

DIYcouture

Couture and human creativity

A small number of high fashion houses in Paris are allowed to call themselves couture. They need to meet strict requirements in order to do so. This exclusivity is part of the identity of haute couture – marking out its value by limiting access. Couture garments have been described as "custom sewn *for a select group of women who can afford them.*"[1.] In fact, if the element of exclusivity through cost is stripped away, the core of couture clothing is that it is custom sewn.

Couture clothing is clothing which is personally designed and individually fitted. As one couture house states, "the couturier's ultimate gift, [is] that of being able to create wonderfully original ideas that... reflect the wearer's personality."[2.] Perhaps it is too much to claim that clothing reflects personality, but it is indeed a gift to be able to make clothing that meets the wearer's tastes, outside of what is currently 'in fashion.'

And anyone can make for themselves. It is possible to adopt the role of designer and maker. A piece of hand-made clothing becomes 'exclusive' only to the extent that it is a one-off; it is exclusive to the maker because their thoughts and ideas have been focused on it for a period of time, and produced a unique outcome.

Becoming a designer and maker simply requires an understanding of the construction process, a process that traditional sewing patterns often render inaccessible through specialist terminology and through complicated layouts. Sewing is a visual activity and it makes sense to learn how to do it with visual guidance. DIYcouture seeks to demystify the construction process.

It is the ability to create that DIYcouture holds in most high esteem. Humans are makers before we are consumers. Although "capital seeks to solidify its power and profit over the existential needs of people to make themselves out of their own labour, intelligence and creativity,"[3.] humans continue to be busy with our hands; to make, to give, to swap and to share.

Seeing backwards

Because DIYcouture respects making, it holds in high esteem the hands that form the history behind each of the garments we buy on the high street. Of course, these are mostly not produced in couture houses in Paris, but on production lines scattered globally, which come and go according to the fluctuating whims of trends and markets.

There are hands all over the world engaged in the production of clothing that flies off the shelves faster than it was made. On the whole, "the international visibility of the producers of real goods is eclipsed by the sartorial glow of the commodity."[4.] But even as chains of production become more complex, as processes are split and atomised and individual instances of making, which produce a whole, are divided across country borders, the desire to unpick objects – to take them back along the chain and understand where they came from – seems to be thriving.

DIYcouture would like to take part in making what is usually invisible visible; to bring it up out of the well, hauling it up so it exists above ground. By going through the motions of garment production, we can transport ourselves into a thousand different pairs of shoes that carry out the same actions as we do, and bring the beginning

---

[1.] p. 07 *Couture Sewing Techniques* by Claire B Shaeffer

[2.] http://www.normanhartnell.com/house_style.html

[3.] p. 05, 'Piecework: Home, Factory, Studio, Exhibit' by Maureen Sherlock, from *The Object Of Labour: Art, Cloth and Cultural Production*

[4.] p. 1 *Ibid.*

of the assembly line closer to home. Perhaps if we physically understand the work that goes into clothing production, we can look backwards from a finished product that we receive and build a sense of value outside of a bargain price tag.

DIYcouture exists because of a belief in making, but also because of an impulse to take things apart. The desire to undo feeds not only the philosophy of DIYcouture but the practical methodology it applies to the making process. You can use your backwards spectacles to unpick the human history of a garment, and also to undo the practical process that built a garment from a flat piece of fabric. If you can see a whole piece of clothing and learn to undo it in your mind, then you can learn the making process. Clothes are made like cardboard boxes are made – by binding the edges of large flat shapes together. You can rewind a garment, just as you can flatten a cardboard box, and through undoing you can learn how to put together.

DIYcouture encourages you to use its series of books to understand the basics of garment construction so that you can demystify clothes making, and also to learn to look at a piece of clothing and mentally deconstruct it, so that you can learn to undo and 're'-make any piece of clothing you see.

Time and freedom

Of course, being able to buy a whole garment – the end product of a process – gives us freedom: the freedom to spend our time in other ways, rather than in making clothes. Making a garment requires some planning and some patience – it meets none of the desires that seek satisfaction through 'retail therapy.' DIYcouture hopes in a small way to slow down the process of consumption, helping people to produce long-lasting garments that are precious, rather than disposable. Fashion implicitly retains its obsession with what is new and what is next. As time *does* pass, an obsession with the new inevitably creates the unfashionable, which becomes waste. DIYcouture hopes to help build a physical antithesis of fast-fashion.

Being able to make a garment from start to finish gives us a sort of luxurious freedom too. This is the freedom to be in control of a whole production process - to see something through from start to finish. Our day to day existence is influenced by dissociative fragmentation, which takes away "the satisfactions associated with planning and practical skills that lead to a finished job, not just a partial one." [5] If you have intellectual control over production, you are not just a consumer, you are a human that decides, thinks and makes.

[5] p. 16, 'Piecework: Home, Factory, Studio, Exhibit' by Maureen Sherlock, from *The Object Of Labour: Art, Cloth and Cultural Production*

Clothes-making equipment

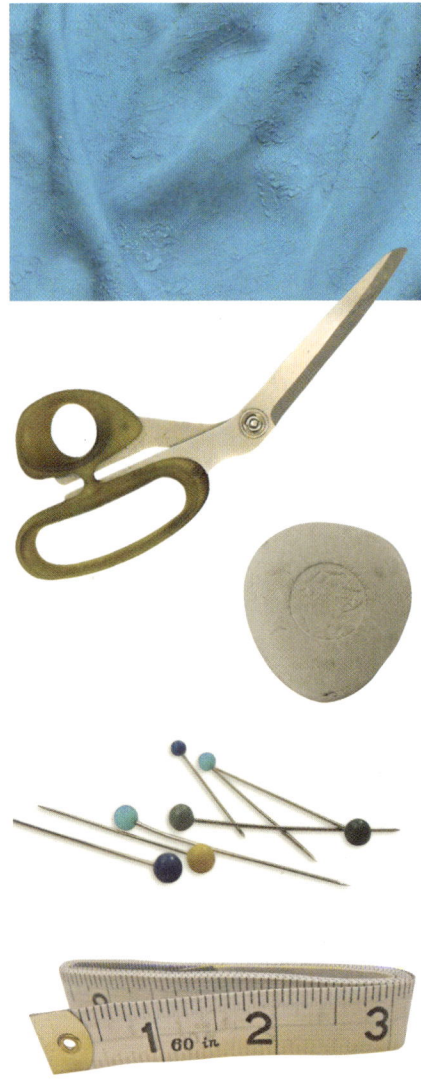

There are a few items you need in order to make clothes. These are:

Fabric – The amount of fabric you need for the pleated skirt will depend on your size and on what kind of skirt you are making. You may be making a mini skirt, or a skirt that brushes the floor. Have a look at pages 12-13 before you buy your fabric, so that you can estimate how much you will use.

Fabric scissors – Get yourself a pair of fabric scissors. Cheap ones will work fine and more expensive ones will probably last you forever. Look after your scissors - don't cut paper with them, it will blunt the blades, which will start snagging your fabric.

Tailors chalk – You can get tailors chalk in the form of a big flat soapy triangle as pictured or as a pencil. Either will do. Tailors chalk allows you to make marks onto your fabric that easily brush or wash off. Rub the tailors chalk on in short, firm strokes whilst pressing the fabric down with your free hand to hold it securely.

Pins – You need a few pins, the sharper the better. When pinning, position your pins at right angles to the edge of the fabric. It is better not to sew over your pins, but if you sew over a pin pinned at a right angle your needle has a greater chance of not snapping.

Tape measure – Any tape measure will work, as long as it has numbers :)

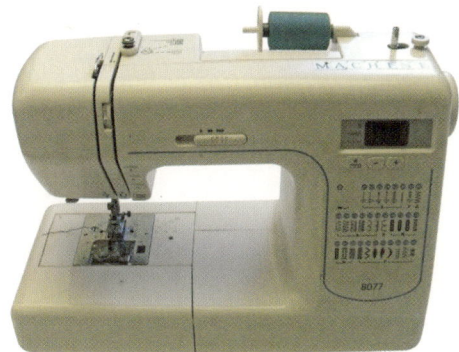

Sewing machine – You can make professional garments with just two stitches, straight and zig-zag, which are the two most basic stitches found on nearly all sewing machines. You will only need these two stitches to make the pleated skirt. The internet is full of guidance on how to choose a machine. See the links section at www.diy-couture.co.uk for a way into this.

Thread – You need to choose a thread that is a similar colour to your fabric. Take a cutting of fabric into the shop with you when you choose your thread. If you can't find an exact match, choose a thread that is slightly darker than your fabric.

Bobbin – Your sewing machine should come with a few empty bobbins, made of plastic or metal (as pictured). You need to wind thread onto this yourself. Your sewing machine instruction booklet will tell you how to do this.

Quick Unpick – You can't expect to get everything right the first time. Making mistakes when you sew is frustrating, because it takes three times as long to undo them as it does to make them in the first place. If only you could just Edit-Undo. Until then, you have the quick unpick. Unpicking is a good time to have a gaze out of the window - daylight helps you to see the stitches. Just slip the long metal spike under your unwanted stitch and push. The curved metal edge will slice through your thread. You can just cut every fourth or fifth stitch and pull your fabric gently apart to speed up the process.

Fabric

Fabric is the essence of a garment and enough respect cannot be given to it. Choosing fabric is exciting, as you are being presented with shelves full of possibilities. You can look at each fabric and paint a mental image of your future garment made from this particular textile. It can also be confusing and stressful: you have to choose one possibility from many, homing in on one fabric and ruling out all the others. Quite simply, you have to strike out your intangible dreams and choose your physical reality.

There are two main pointers when it comes to fabric shopping.

1. Get physically involved

More important than having technical knowledge about fabric is having 'a feel' for it. Having 'a feel' isn't something you are either born or not born with, it's something you can develop. To develop 'a feel,' you need to start feeling. When you are in a fabric shop, scan over the fabrics and approach whichever one takes your eye – take a corner of the fabric and rub it between your thumb and fingers. Take the end of it in both hands and give it a couple of sharp tugs, first one way and then the other. Is it stretchy? Does it have any 'give' at all? Is it prickly, rough, soft, brushed, velvety? Unravel a bit of the fabric and let it hang – 'flounce' it with your hand: cup your hand underneath it and lift it up a few times, as if you are guessing the weight of a bag of mushrooms. Does the fabric flop into folds with gravity? Is it stiff? Is it light and floaty?

You will have an idea of what you want from a fabric, so think about this when you are feeling around. The fabric will exert its own properties onto the garment that you make, and you have to accommodate its wishes. Do you want your skirt/top/dress to flop in folds, to cling to your body, or to stick out stiffly? Do you want the garment to look innocent and delicate, or durable and hardy? Do you want a futuristic feel or something more organic and rustic? Fabric will dictate all of this.

2. Ask questions

Fabric shop staff are usually very knowledgeable about their stock, and often have a fondness for it too. Ask them questions – they will most likely give you more information than you thought you needed. You can ask them what the fabric is called, how wide the roll is, its washing/drying properties and where it comes from. Ask them whether they think it is suitable for what you intend to make. If you happen to like an expensive fabric, they can probably tell you why it is expensive e.g. it is pure silk produced by a unique herd of seventeen intelligent silk worms, hand spun and woven by monks in a village in the Himalayas. Sometimes fabric is expensive because it is 'designer' fabric. By asking questions you can start to tie together what you learn about fabric from feeling it and the more formal/tangible facts about fabric and its properties.

Throughout this book there are pictures of models wearing the different versions of the pleated skirt made from a range of fabrics. Page nine talks a bit about the differences between these skirts and may help you understand how fabric, as well as structural differences, can change the overall appearance of the garment.

In general, life is simpler if you avoid using extremely heavy (e.g thick denim) or extremely light-weight (e.g. chiffon or organza) fabrics. Some sewing machines may struggle to sew thicker fabrics and your needles may snap. Thin fabrics take some skill and delicacy to manipulate, and sometimes your machine will chew up the fabric or snag on the fibres, causing the fabric to wrinkle up irreversibly.

Fabric and fairtrade

At the moment, it is pretty unusual to find fairtrade, organic or recycled fabric in high street fabric shops. Where organic fabric is available, colours are often limited. There is, however, constant innovation in the textiles industry and as a result, a wide range of planet and people friendly fabrics do exist. There are links to some of these on the DIYcouture website at www.diy-couture.co.uk. Hopefully these will become increasingly available to the individual clothes-maker.

Ask the staff at your local fabric shops whether they have considered stocking fairtrade – maybe you can influence their decision as to whether to stock it in the future.

Pleated skirt

This skirt is a pleated skirt that can sit on either the waist or the hips.

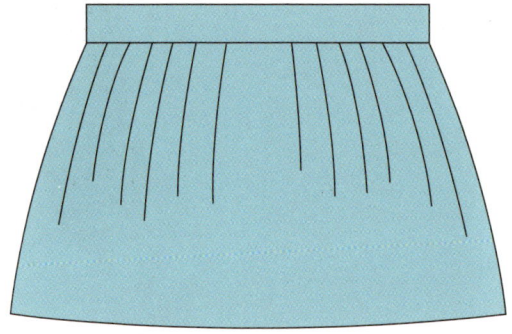

In its most basic form it is made of four pieces of fabric – two for the skirt and two for the waist band.

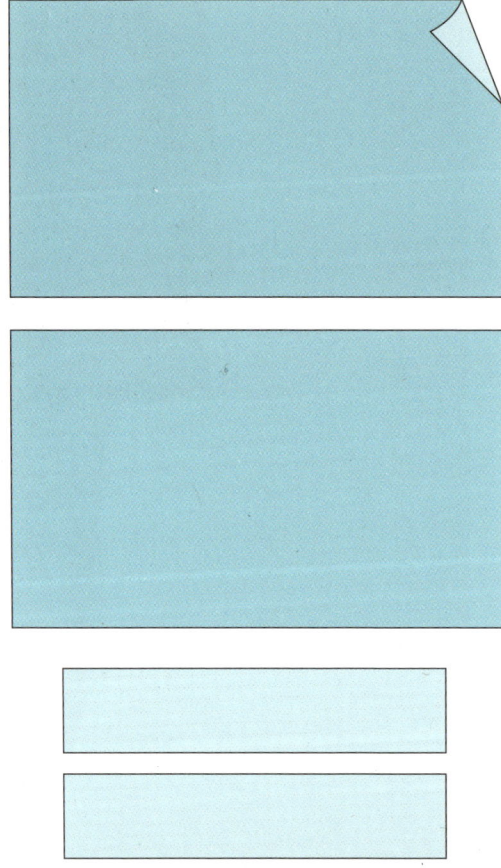

It fastens with a zip and a hook and eye at one side.

Variations

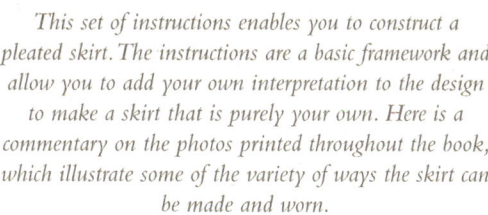

This set of instructions enables you to construct a pleated skirt. The instructions are a basic framework and allow you to add your own interpretation to the design to make a skirt that is purely your own. Here is a commentary on the photos printed throughout the book, which illustrate some of the variety of ways the skirt can be made and worn.

The skirt on p.7 is made from African printed cotton. It is good quality cotton so fairly thick and slightly stiff, holding its shape away from the body.

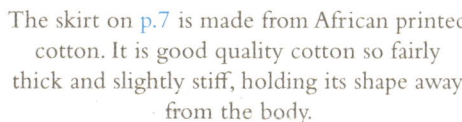

The cyan skirt on p.10-p.11 and pictured throughout the book is made of medium-weight, textured, synthetic fabric which is fairly floppy.

The skirt on p.15 is made of thick polyester, with a glossy shine on just one side. It is a fairly springy fabric that holds its shape, falling in large rounded pleats. The skirt is sewn inwards at the bottom of each of the two side seams so that it doesn't flare out. It has a broad waistband and is very short, increasing the appearance of long legs.

The skirt on p.19 is made of a fairly thin polycotton with two pairs of pleats at the front called 'box pleats'. It is cut at knee length, giving a fairly conservative appearance. It could also look good sitting on the hips.

The big green skirt on p.21 is made of a very light, papery, printed silk from India that feels almost like waterproof tent material and drifts into position. The model wears it with a netted petticoat underneath, which gives it shape.

The skirt on p.29 is made of three different fabrics. Two colours make up the main body of the skirt and a third forms the waistband. The skirt pictured on p.44 is also made of multiple fabrics joined in horizontal stripes. The possibility of joining fabrics together to form the skirt provides endless possibilities to play with.

The floor length skirt on p.26 is made using lycra, which is not a thick fabric but is weighty and flops down with gravity so that the skirt hangs down, sitting against the hips.

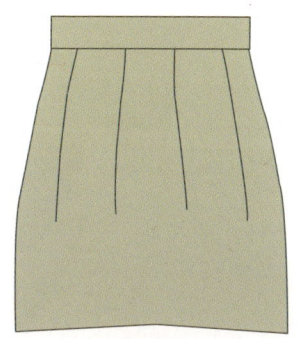

The black and white skirt on p.27 is made of a stiff synthetic fabric that has almost a foamy, cardboardy quality to it, causing it to flare out and hold its shape.

The skirt on p.41 is made of basic black polycotton and is finished with yellow bias binding, providing a striking contrast. Bias binding gives a professional finish and removes the need to make a hem.

First, you need to cut two rectangles that will form the body of your skirt.

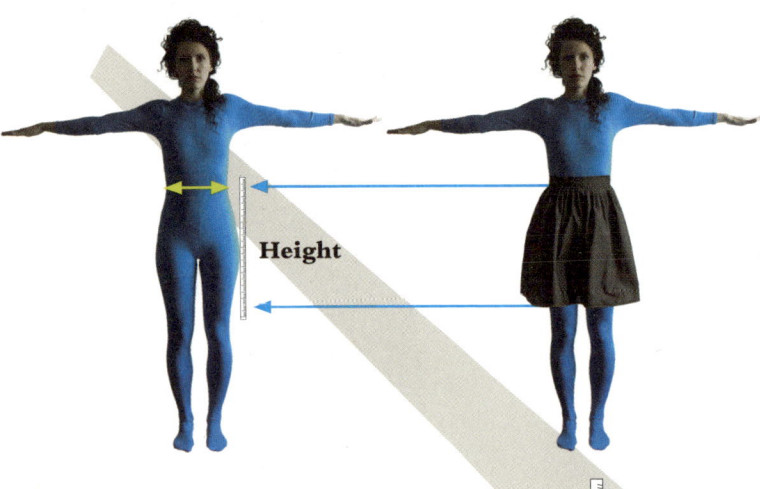

You need to mark the height and width of one rectangle onto your fabric with pins. The **height** of your rectangle should be the same as the length you wish your skirt to be Measure from your waist - or wherever you want your skirt to sit - down your leg to the place you want the skirt to hang. Take a note of this measurement, then add 3cm to it. This extra fabric will allow you to make a hem and a seam later on. Mark this length along one edge of your fabric with a pin.

To decide the **width** of your rectangles, you need to know the distance *across* your waist (or hips or wherever your skirt will sit), how many pleats you wish to make and how big each pleat will be. Use the table on the opposite page to help you keep track of all these numbers. Most importantly, don't worry too much about absolute accuracy, you can always make changes as you go.

Firstly, measure the full distance around your waist, then divide this measurement by two. This number is the distance across your waist, marked on the girl in the top left corner with a yellow double headed arrow. Add 3cm to this to allow for seams. We will call this number your waist measurment.

The measurements that produce the cyan skirt, pictured throughout the book...

The skirt photographed throughout this book has 12 pleats across the front and 12 across the back. The type of pleating used is called knife pleating, where all the pleats lie in the same direction. The pleats here are not strictly uniformly even, but each pleat takes up roughly 5cm of fabric, so 60cm (12 x 5cm) was added to the initial waist measurement to cut the correct size rectangle for this skirt.

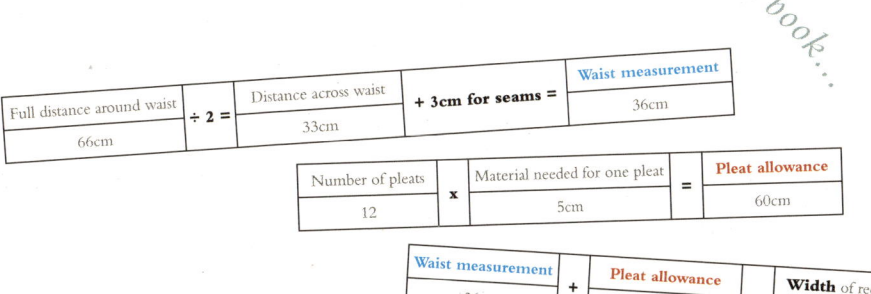

Full distance around waist	÷ 2 =	Distance across waist	+ 3cm for seams =	Waist measurement
66cm		33cm		36cm

Number of pleats	x	Material needed for one pleat	=	Pleat allowance
12		5cm		60cm

Waist measurement	+	Pleat allowance	=	Width of rectangle
36cm		60cm		96cm

Blank tables to help you work out the width your rectangle needs to be...

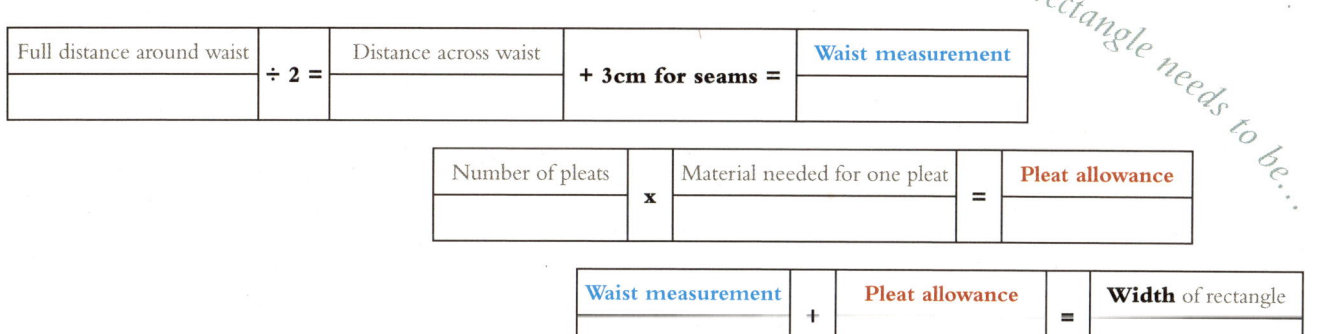

Full distance around waist	÷ 2 =	Distance across waist	+ 3cm for seams =	Waist measurement

Number of pleats	x	Material needed for one pleat	=	Pleat allowance

Waist measurement	+	Pleat allowance	=	Width of rectangle

You need to add additional fabric to this measurement to allow for your pleats. Have a look at p.16-p.19 to help you decide how many and how big your pleats will be and write these figures down in the second blank table. Add the pleat allowance to the waist measurement. This is the width your rectangle needs to be :) - mark this measurement onto your fabric with a pin.

Use a sheet of newspaper as a guide to cut straight lines. Once you have cut your first rectangle, rest it on top of your fabric and use it as a template to cut your second piece exactly the same shape. You now have two identical rectangles.

Zig-zag stitch along all the edges of your two rectangles.

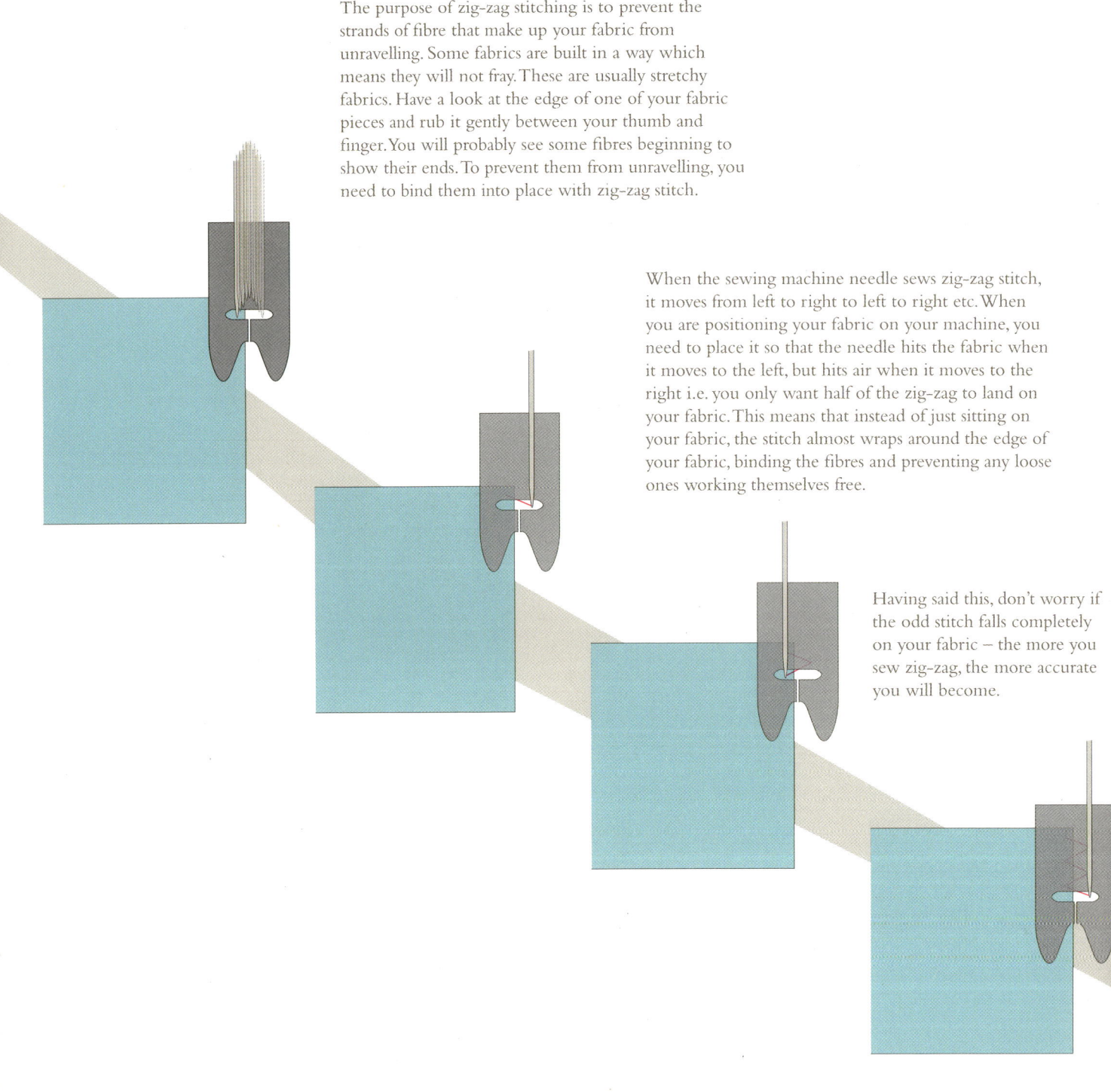

The purpose of zig-zag stitching is to prevent the strands of fibre that make up your fabric from unravelling. Some fabrics are built in a way which means they will not fray. These are usually stretchy fabrics. Have a look at the edge of one of your fabric pieces and rub it gently between your thumb and finger. You will probably see some fibres beginning to show their ends. To prevent them from unravelling, you need to bind them into place with zig-zag stitch.

When the sewing machine needle sews zig-zag stitch, it moves from left to right to left to right etc. When you are positioning your fabric on your machine, you need to place it so that the needle hits the fabric when it moves to the left, but hits air when it moves to the right i.e. you only want half of the zig-zag to land on your fabric. This means that instead of just sitting on your fabric, the stitch almost wraps around the edge of your fabric, binding the fibres and preventing any loose ones working themselves free.

Having said this, don't worry if the odd stitch falls completely on your fabric – the more you sew zig-zag, the more accurate you will become.

Next you are going to make your pleats.

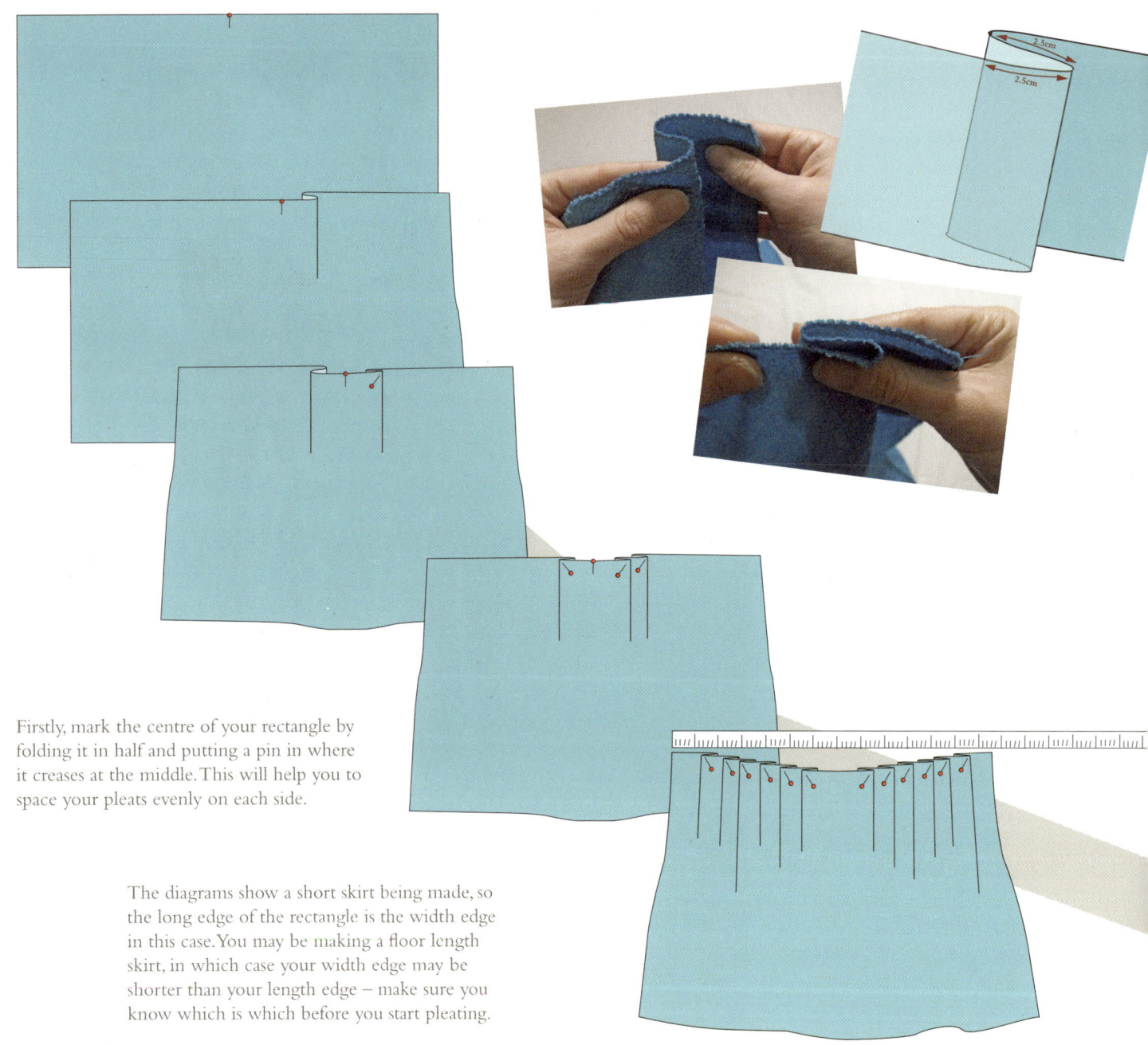

Firstly, mark the centre of your rectangle by folding it in half and putting a pin in where it creases at the middle. This will help you to space your pleats evenly on each side.

The diagrams show a short skirt being made, so the long edge of the rectangle is the width edge in this case. You may be making a floor length skirt, in which case your width edge may be shorter than your length edge – make sure you know which is which before you start pleating.

Make your first pleat to one side of the centre and pin it into place. Make the equivalent pleat on the other side of the centre (a mirror image of your first). Keep pinning your pleats into place until you have made as many as you planned. Make sure you have about 4cm of unpleated fabric at each side of your skirt piece.

Before you sew the pleats into place, measure the pleated edge and check that it is at least as long as the waist measurement you wrote down. If it is smaller, unpin a pleat at each side. Sew over your pinned pleats with a line of straight stitch running about 1cm away from the edge. For tips on straight stitch see the following page.

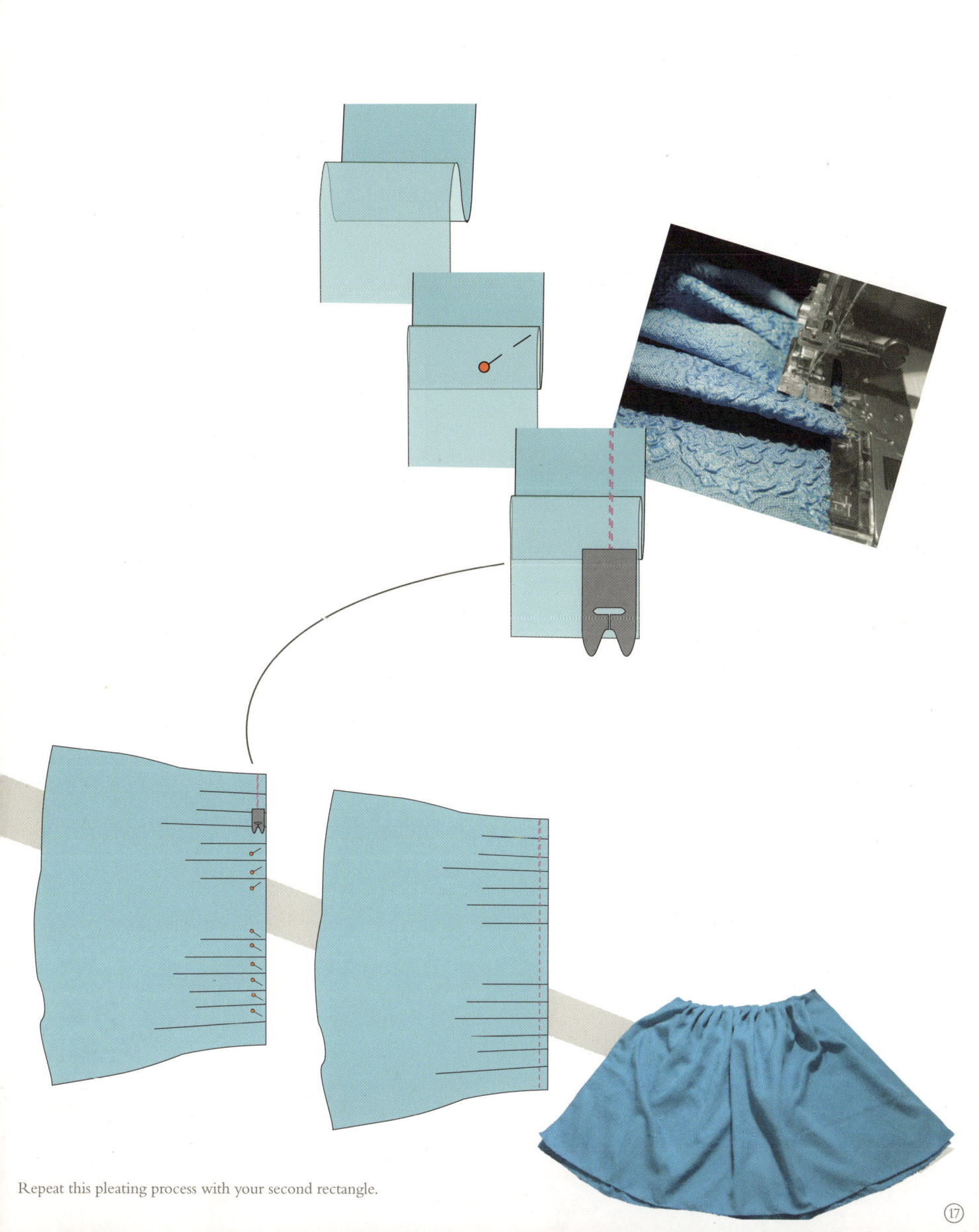

Repeat this pleating process with your second rectangle.

You can pleat your skirt in different ways.

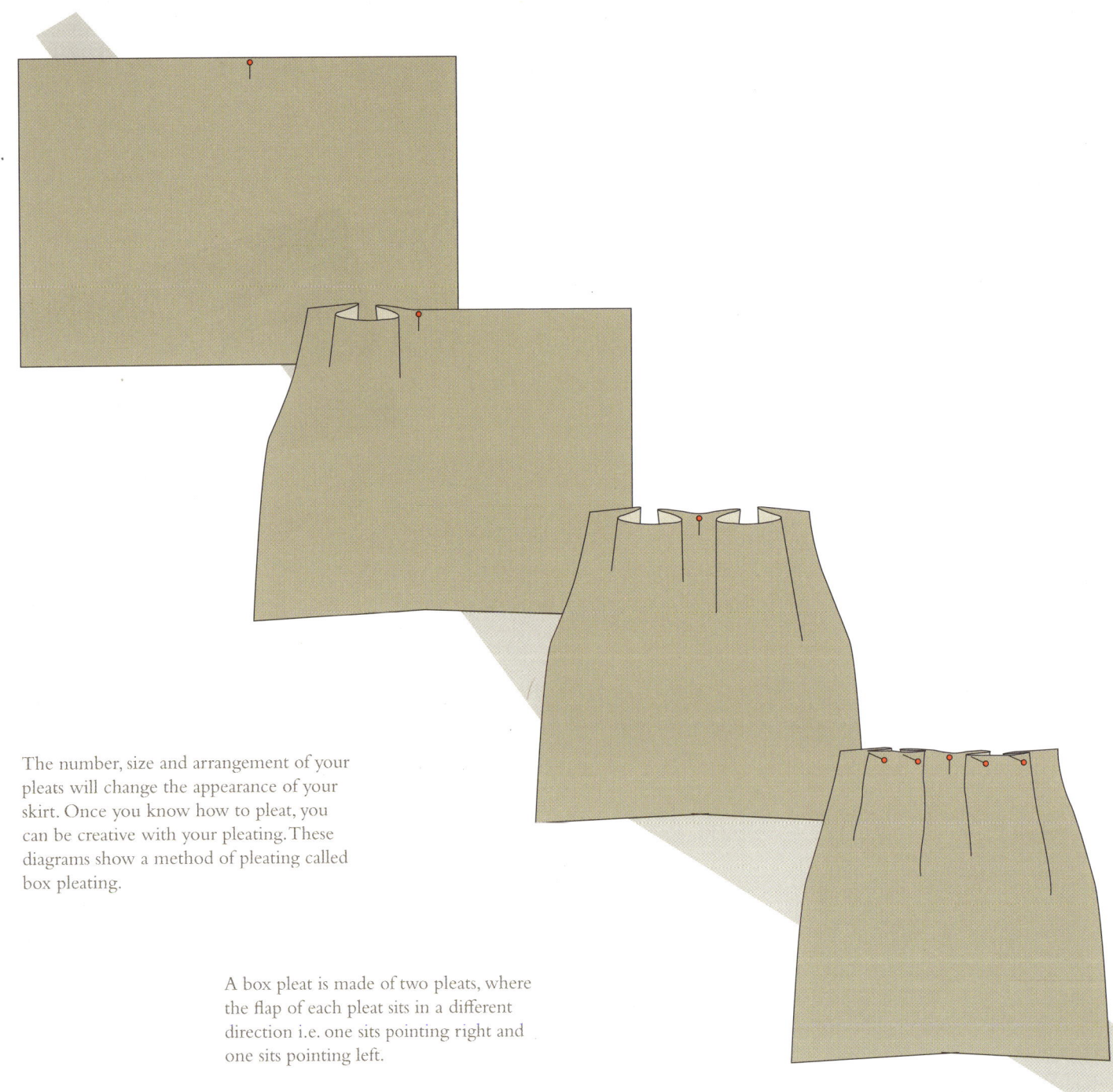

The number, size and arrangement of your pleats will change the appearance of your skirt. Once you know how to pleat, you can be creative with your pleating. These diagrams show a method of pleating called box pleating.

A box pleat is made of two pleats, where the flap of each pleat sits in a different direction i.e. one sits pointing right and one sits pointing left.

Again, mark the centre point of your rectangle with a pin so that you can make your pleats equidistant from the centre on each side. Fold and pin your pleats into position then turn your skirt and sew the pleats securely with a line of straight stitch running about 1cm away from the edge.

Straight stitch.

When your machine sews straight stitch, it is simply pushing thread in and out of your fabric in a long line. If you were to pull at the thread at one end of your row of stitching you could begin to work it loose. You need to prevent this from happening and can do so very simply.

Your machine sews naturally 'forwards', towards you, as if it is gently chomping your fabric and excreting it out behind it. Whenever you begin a row of straight stitch you will naturally wish to start sewing right at the far edge of your fabric. However, you need to position your needle about 2cm 'inland'. With your needle so positioned, put your machine-foot down and set your machine to sew backwards. Gently cover this distance in reverse with a short line of straight stitch.

When your needle is at the far edge of the fabric, you can begin to sew forwards, directly over the line you have just sewn. This will hold the stitches in position and ensure you are making strong, long lasting garments.

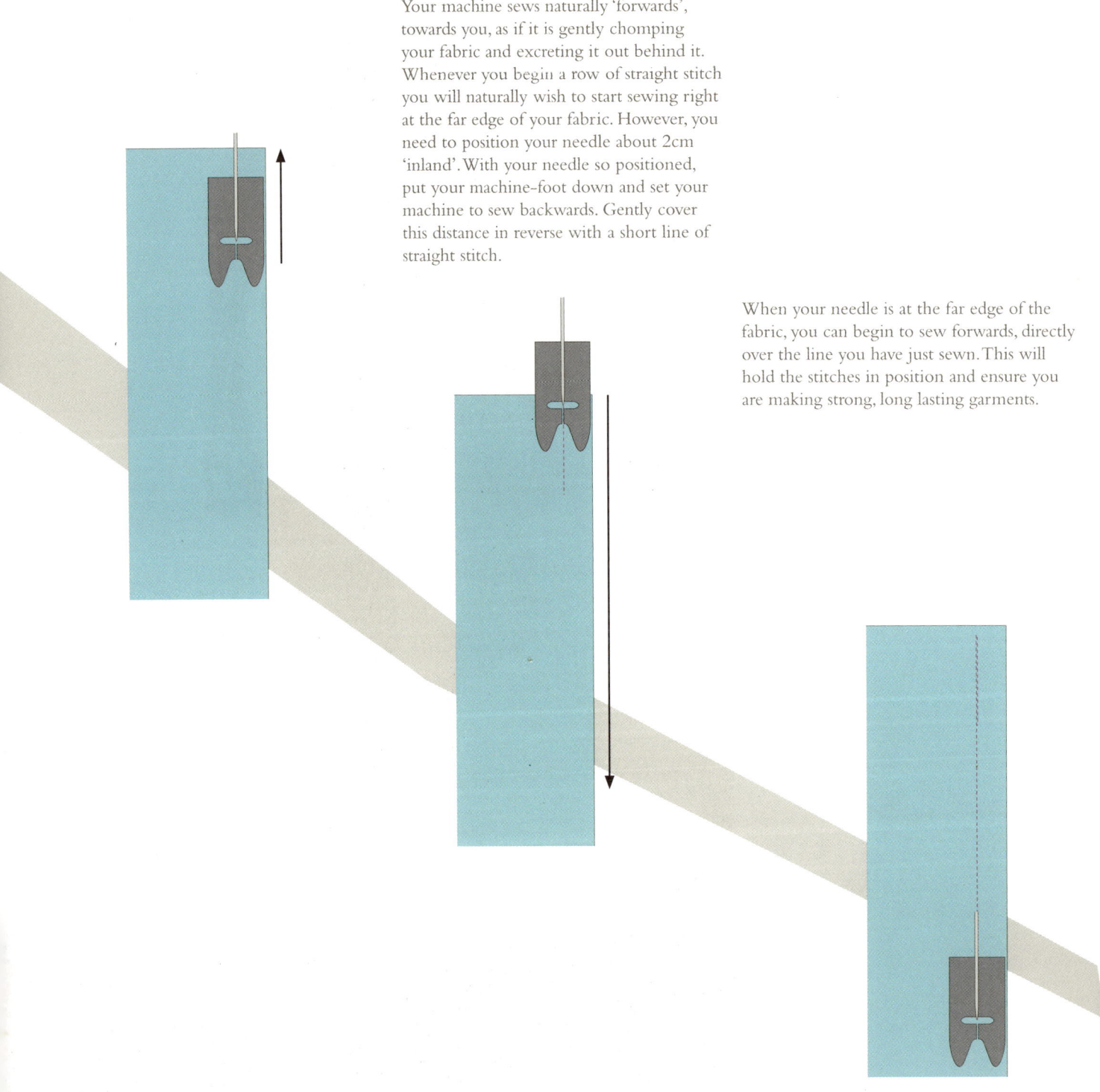

Now you are going to join the front and back of your skirt.

...Before you do so, hold one of your pieces up to your waist unpick the pleats that take it to the size you want and trim

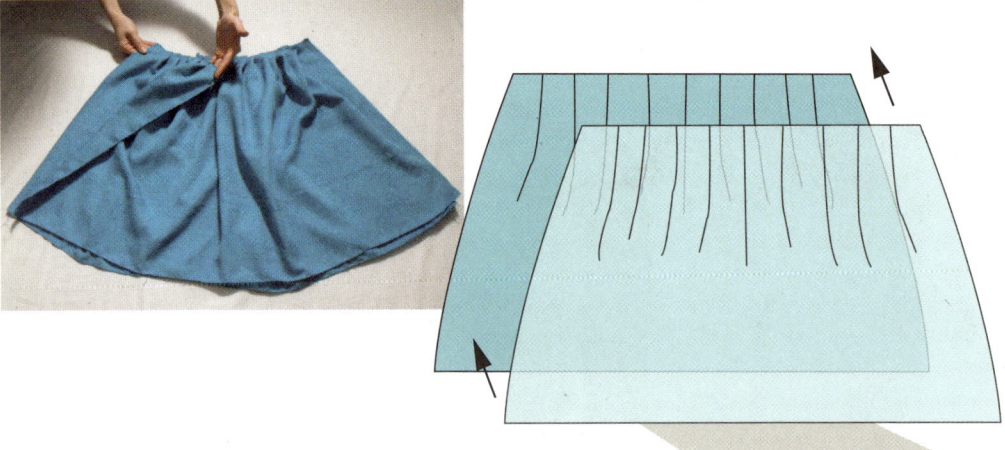

Lay one piece out with the right side of the fabric facing upwards towards you and lay the other piece on top of it, with the right side facing down. You should be looking at the wrong side of your fabric.

You are going to sew the two pieces together up each of the vertical sides, but not *all* the way up each of these edges.

On one side you need to leave room for a zip. On the other, you need to leave about 6cm to give yourself some room to manoeuvre when you attach your waistband later on.

Take your zip and lie it next to your skirt. Jam a pair of pins into your fabric at the bottom of your zip. These act as a warning, to remind yourself to stop sewing when you get to this point. Carry on pinning down this side. Pin up the other side and again, remind yourself with a couple of pins where to stop (about 6cm from the top).

heck that the fabric is the right width. If it is too small, unpick a pleat at each end. If it's far too big, own. If there is only a bit of excess fabric you can leave it and trim it off further down the line...

Sew up each side of the skirt with a line of straight stitch, stopping when you get to the pairs of warning pins.

You need to neaten up the unjoined edges you have left to accommodate your zip.

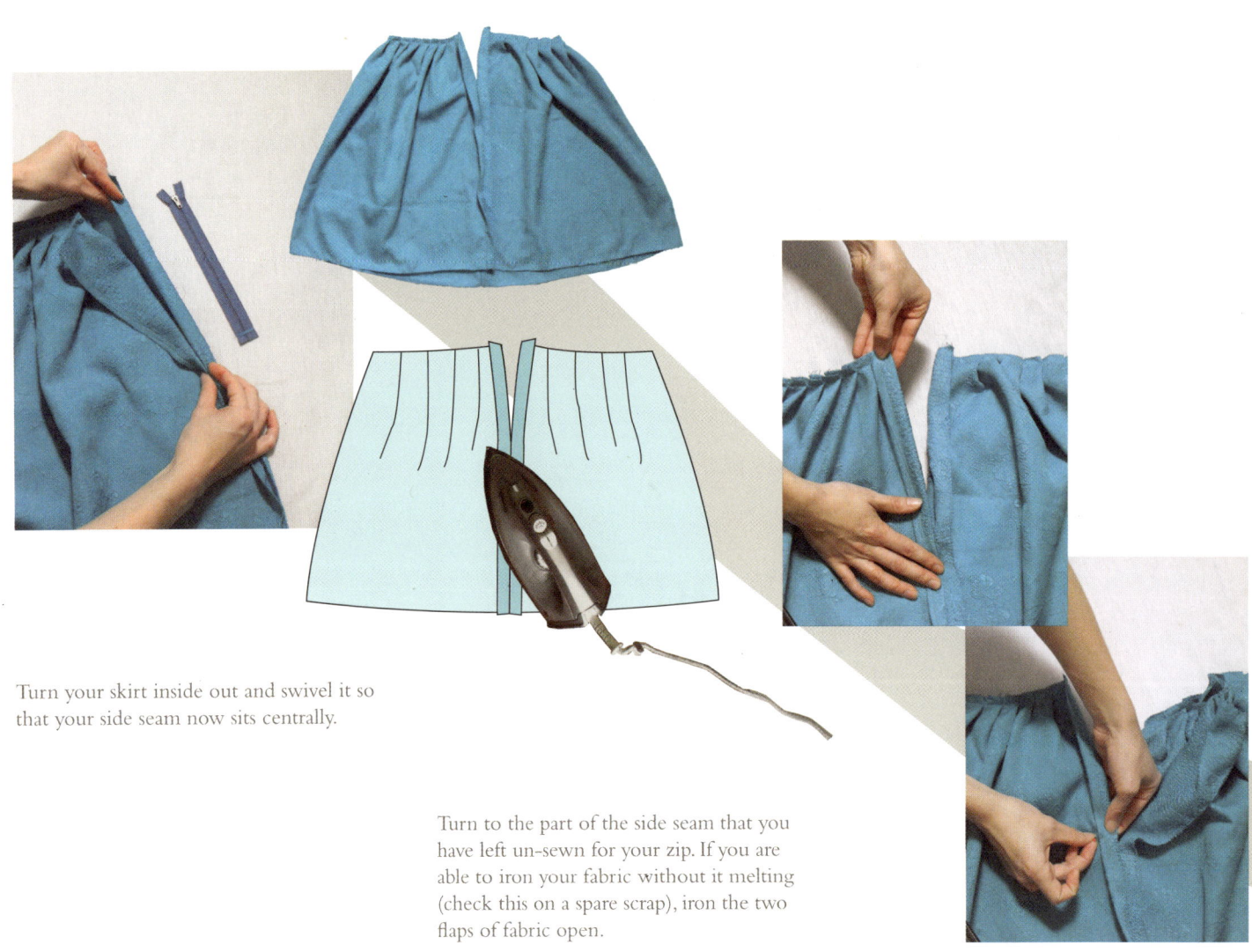

Turn your skirt inside out and swivel it so that your side seam now sits centrally.

Turn to the part of the side seam that you have left un-sewn for your zip. If you are able to iron your fabric without it melting (check this on a spare scrap), iron the two flaps of fabric open.

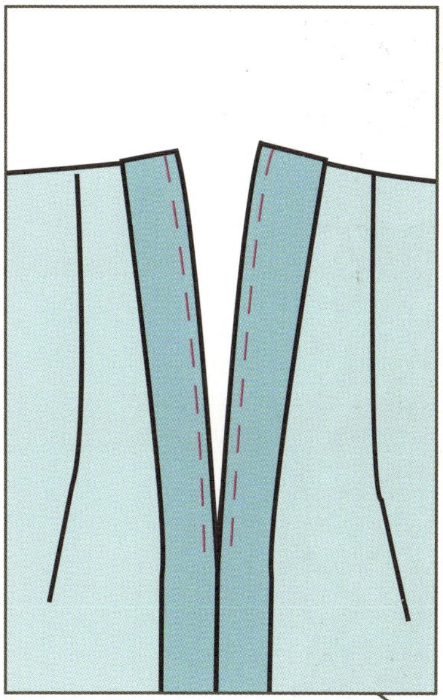

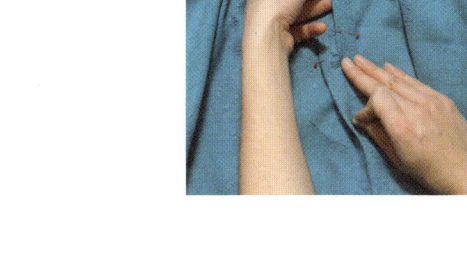

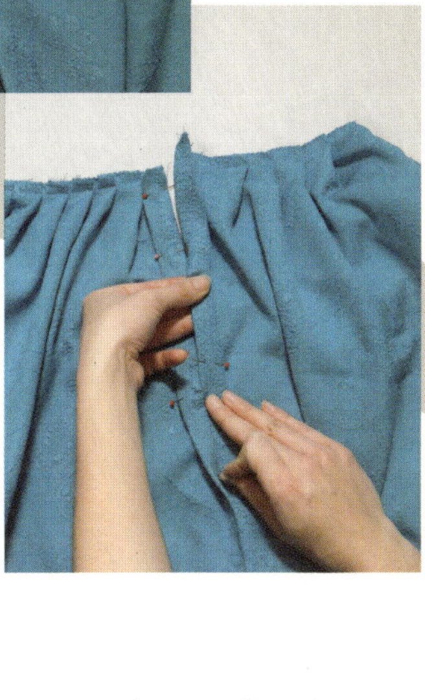

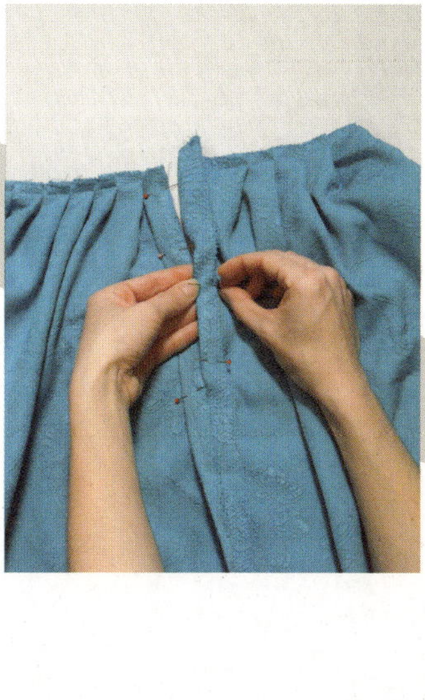

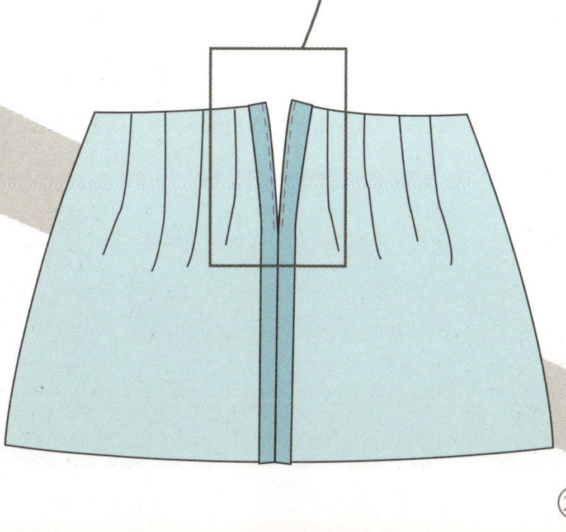

Pin these flaps open and secure them into place with a line of straight stitch running 2 or 3 mm away from the folded edge

Now you are going to cut the pieces that will form your waistband.

You need to cut two more rectangles of fabric. Firstly, to get an accurate width, lay your skirt out with the waist edge running parallel with one edge of your fabric. Add 3cm to this width and make a mark with a pin or chalk. You will need this extra fabric to fold under to create a neat edge next to your zip.

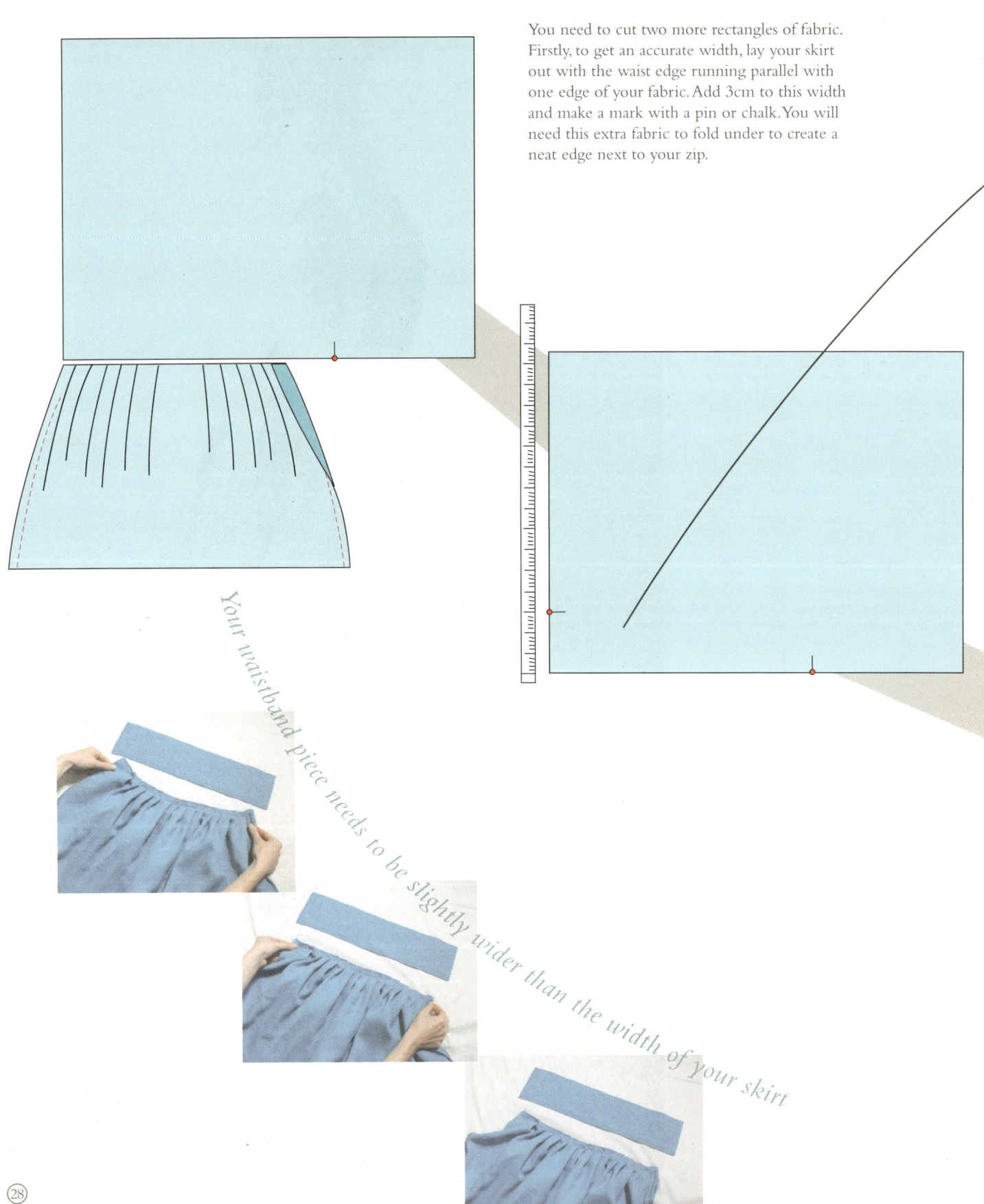

Your waistband piece needs to be slightly wider than the width of your skirt

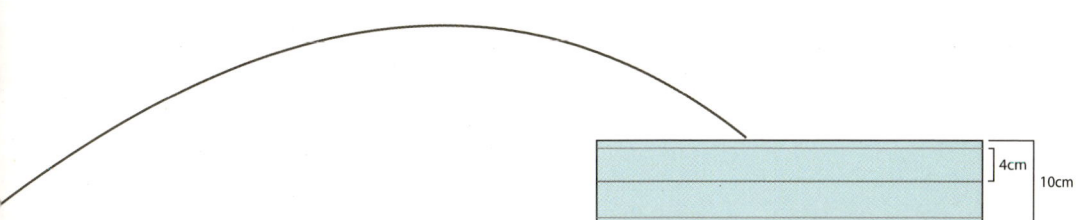

Depth-wise, the pieces should be double the depth that you wish your waist band to be plus 2cm to allow for joins. If you wish your waistband to be 4cm deep, you need to double this - making 8 - then add 2, making 10 in total.

Cut your first rectangle out. You can use newspaper or your tape measure as a guide to help you cut straight lines. Use your first rectangle as a template to cut a second one exactly the same. Zig-zag around all four edges of each of your pieces.

You need to prepare your waistband pieces before joining them to your skirt.

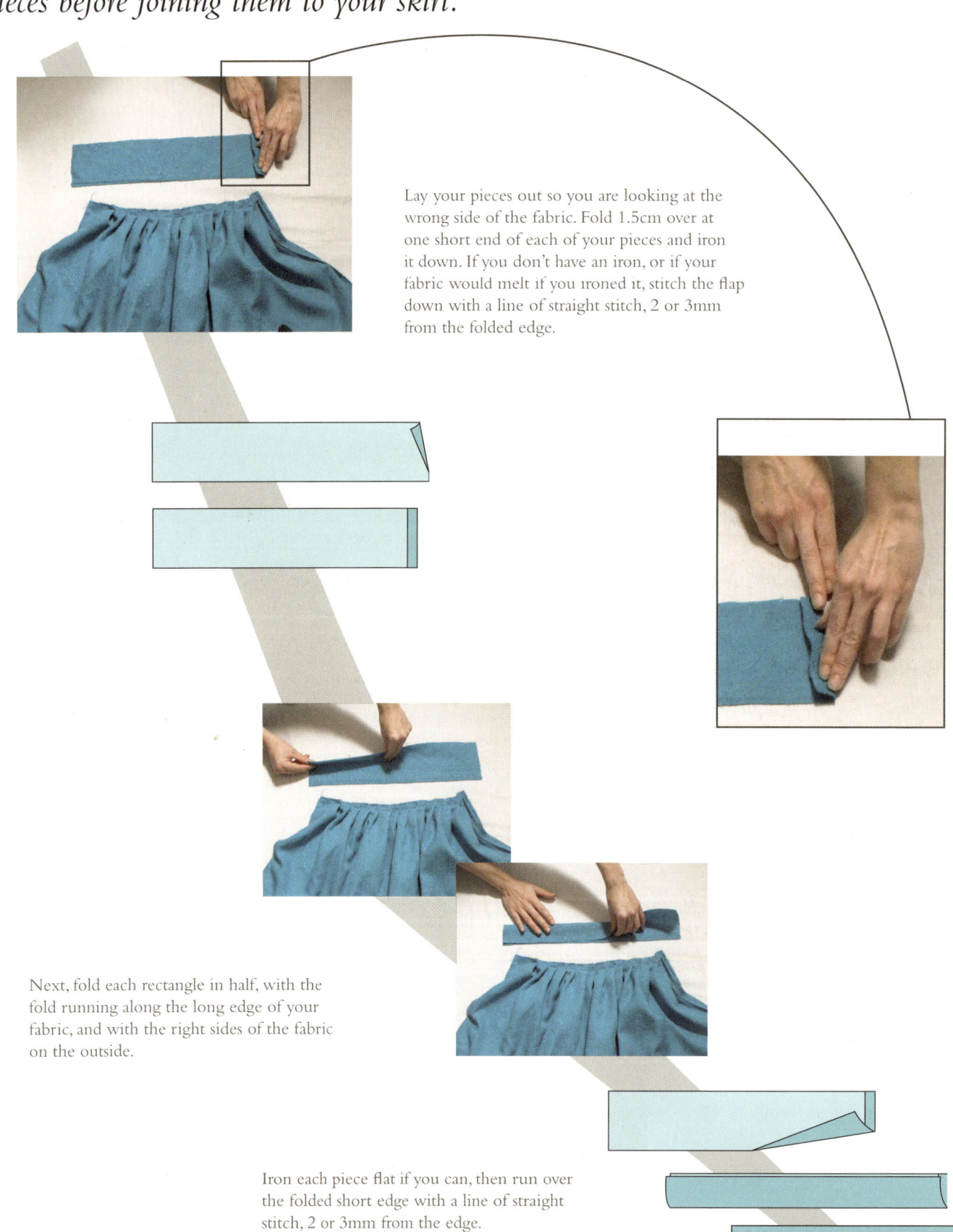

Lay your pieces out so you are looking at the wrong side of the fabric. Fold 1.5cm over at one short end of each of your pieces and iron it down. If you don't have an iron, or if your fabric would melt if you ironed it, stitch the flap down with a line of straight stitch, 2 or 3mm from the folded edge.

Next, fold each rectangle in half, with the fold running along the long edge of your fabric, and with the right sides of the fabric on the outside.

Iron each piece flat if you can, then run over the folded short edge with a line of straight stitch, 2 or 3mm from the edge.

Next you need to position your waistband pieces on your skirt.

Take one waist band piece and lay it on top of the **right** side of one of your skirt pieces. You need to match the hemmed edge of your waistband piece with the neat edge you have made on your skirt for your zip opening.

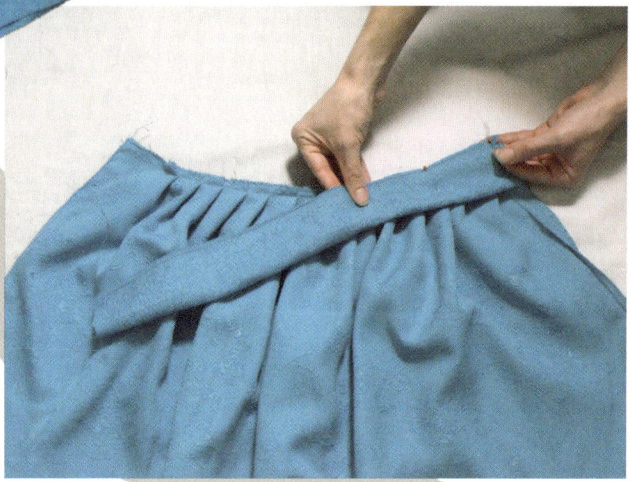

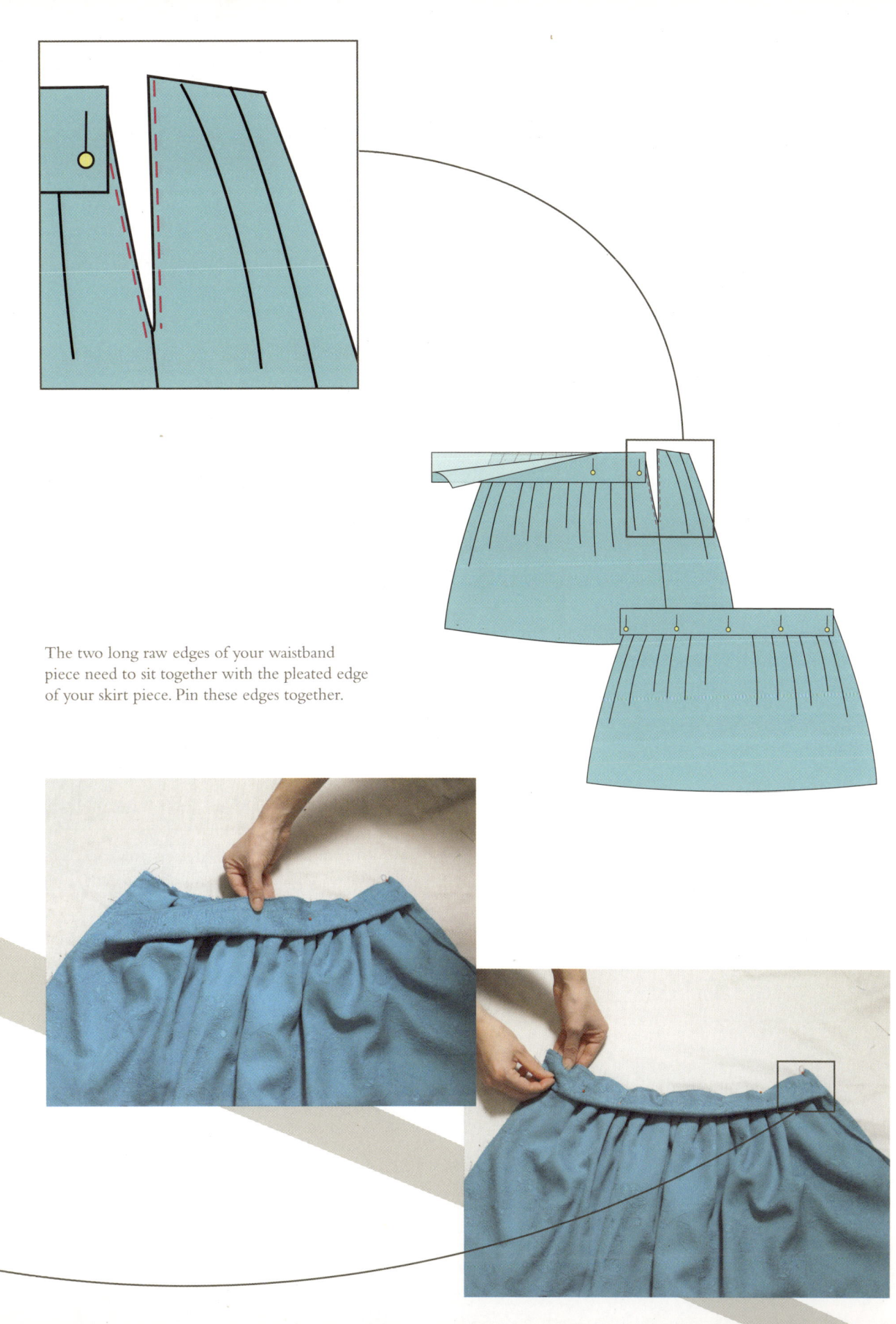

The two long raw edges of your waistband piece need to sit together with the pleated edge of your skirt piece. Pin these edges together.

Now finish off your waistband area.

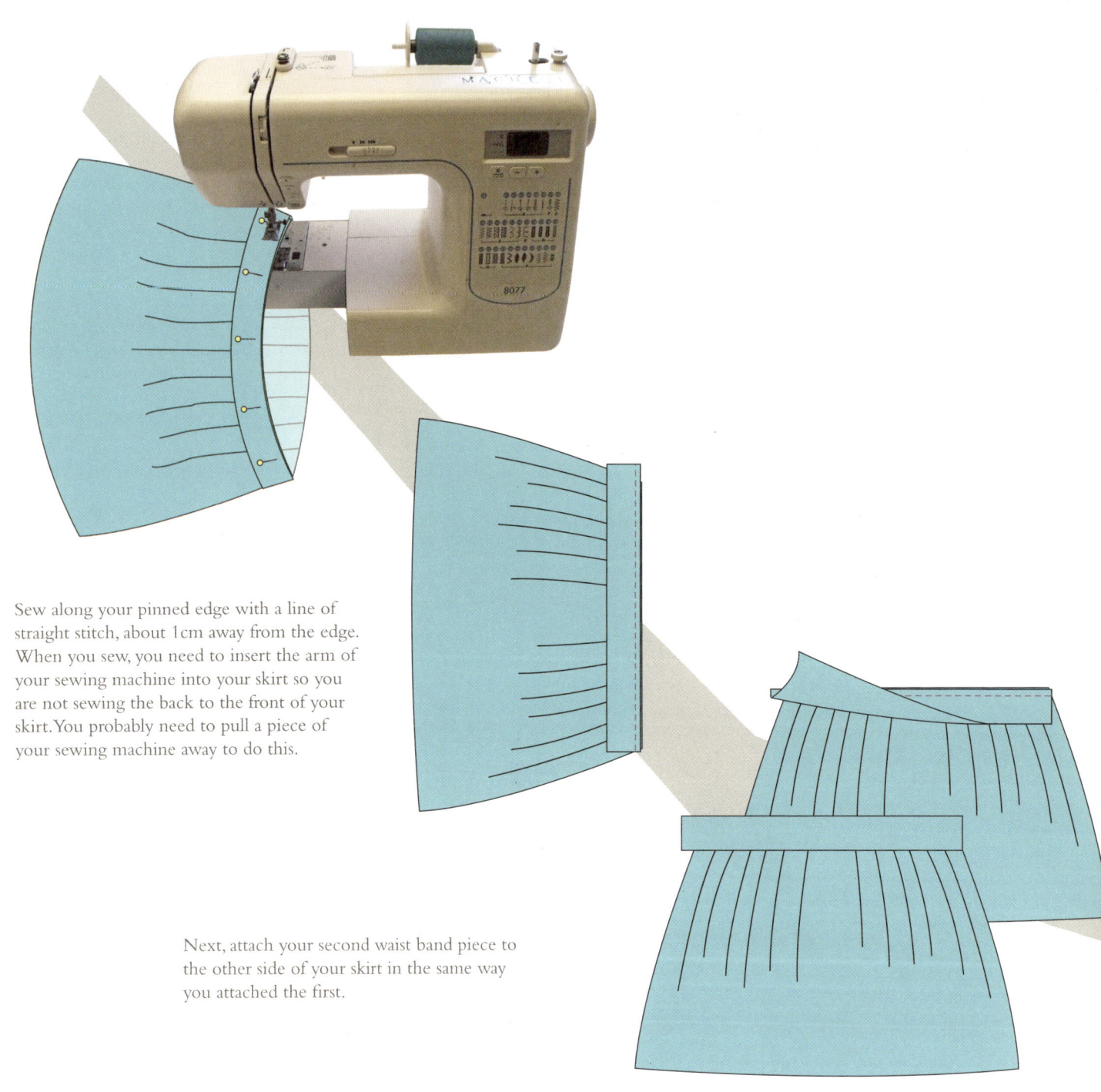

Sew along your pinned edge with a line of straight stitch, about 1cm away from the edge. When you sew, you need to insert the arm of your sewing machine into your skirt so you are not sewing the back to the front of your skirt. You probably need to pull a piece of your sewing machine away to do this.

Next, attach your second waist band piece to the other side of your skirt in the same way you attached the first.

With both waistband pieces attached, flip them upwards so that the zig-zagged edges of your waistband piece and your skirt, which form a flap, are hidden on the inside of your skirt. Then turn your skirt inside out.

Before you sew up the zipless side of your skirt, you need to decide what to do with the flaps of fabric where your waistband joins your skirt.

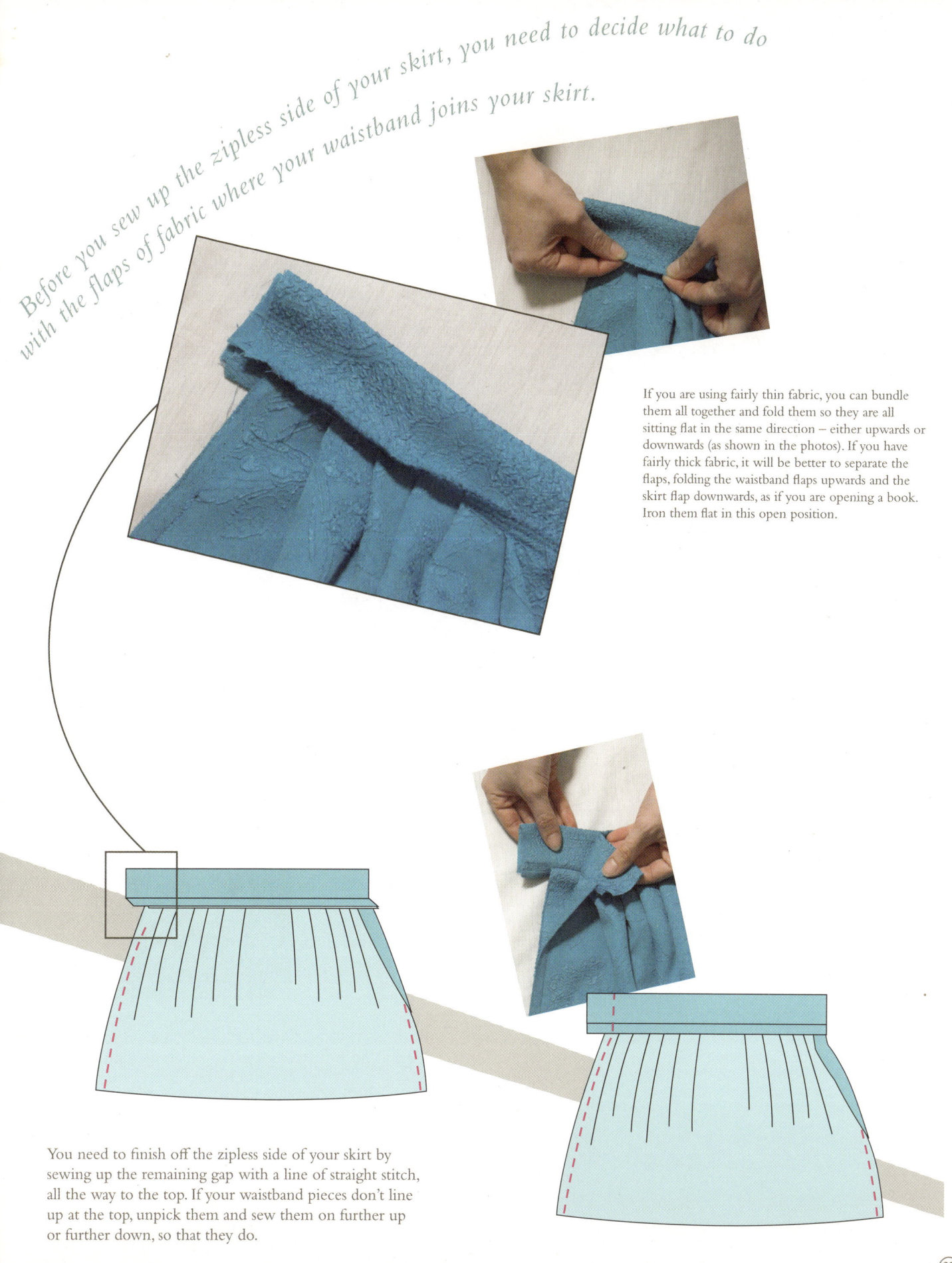

If you are using fairly thin fabric, you can bundle them all together and fold them so they are all sitting flat in the same direction – either upwards or downwards (as shown in the photos). If you have fairly thick fabric, it will be better to separate the flaps, folding the waistband flaps upwards and the skirt flap downwards, as if you are opening a book. Iron them flat in this open position.

You need to finish off the zipless side of your skirt by sewing up the remaining gap with a line of straight stitch, all the way to the top. If your waistband pieces don't line up at the top, unpick them and sew them on further up or further down, so that they do.

You need to pin your zip into the right position.

Turn your skirt so that you are looking at the right side of the fabric – all untidy joins should be hidden away on the inside and your skirt should be looking pretty neat.

Lay your zip under the two neat vertical edges you have made for the zip opening. You need both edges to meet exactly where the teeth of the zip meet. Pin them into position one at a time, lining up the vertical edge with the vertical line where your zip teeth meet.

When the two edges are pinned in place, you shouldn't be able to see your zip :). If you have the patience, it will really help you to roughly hand-stitch your zip into place. Take a coloured thread that contrasts with your fabric, so that you can see it clearly to unpick it, and stitch all the way around your zip. You can make fairly large stitches – about 1cm long. Now you can take your pins out.

Then you need to sew your zip into place.

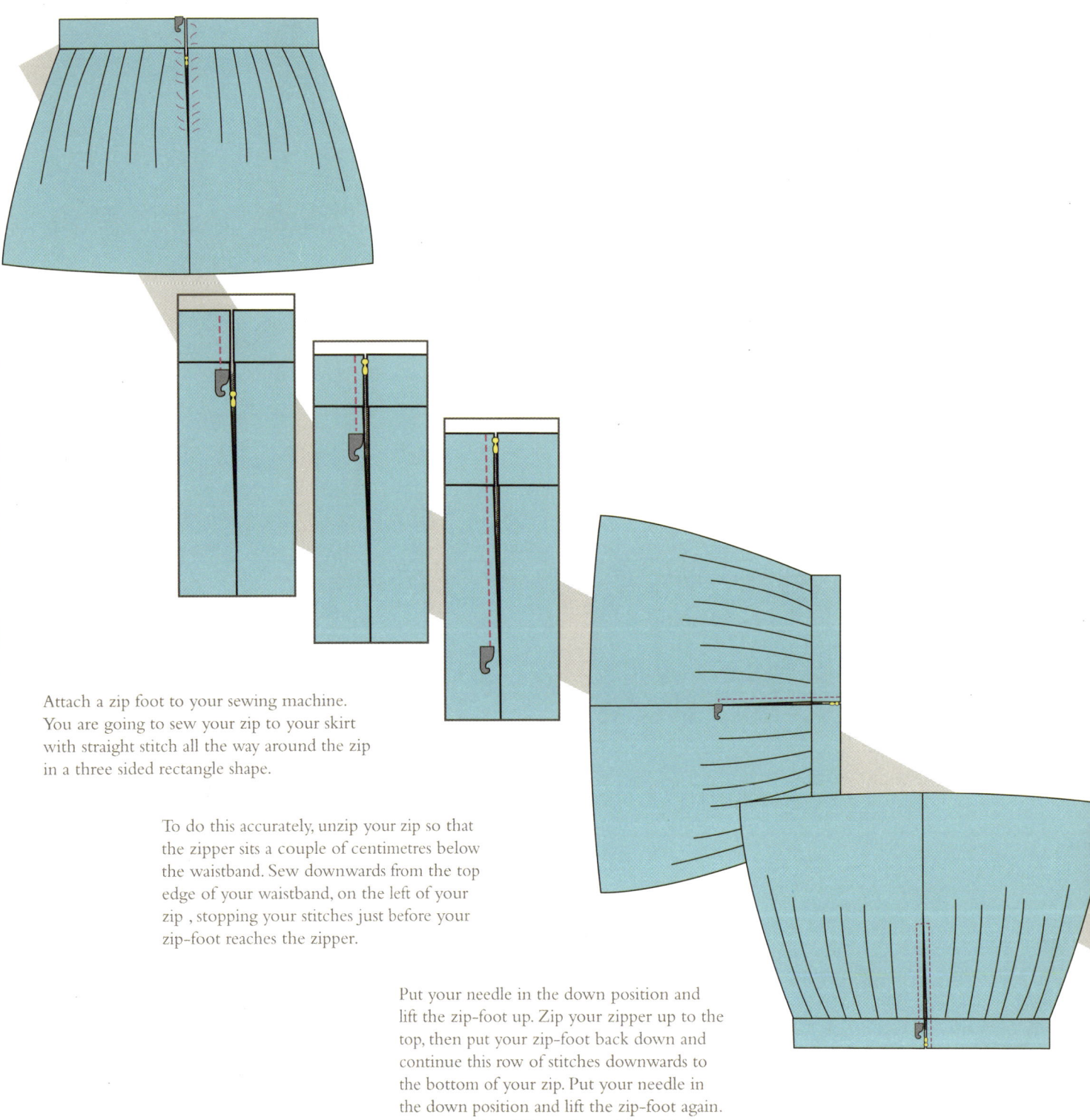

Attach a zip foot to your sewing machine. You are going to sew your zip to your skirt with straight stitch all the way around the zip in a three sided rectangle shape.

To do this accurately, unzip your zip so that the zipper sits a couple of centimetres below the waistband. Sew downwards from the top edge of your waistband, on the left of your zip , stopping your stitches just before your zip-foot reaches the zipper.

Put your needle in the down position and lift the zip-foot up. Zip your zipper up to the top, then put your zip-foot back down and continue this row of stitches downwards to the bottom of your zip. Put your needle in the down position and lift the zip-foot again. Turn your skirt 90º (so the waistband is on the right), put the zip-foot back down again and sew a short row of stitches across the bottom of your zip.

Once again put the needle down, lift the zip-foot and swivel the skirt so that you can sew up the third side of your rectangle, from the bottom to the top of your zip.

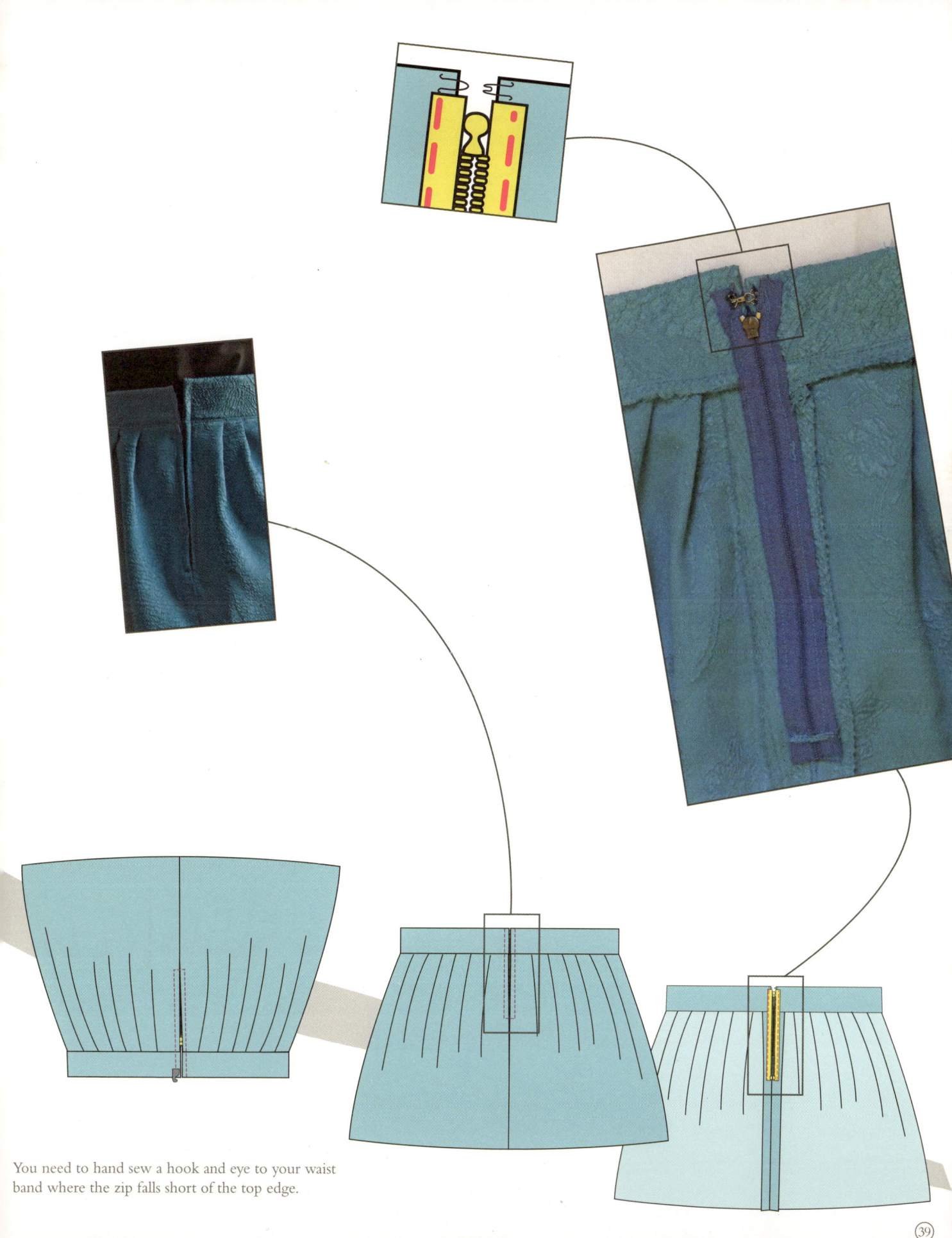

You need to hand sew a hook and eye to your waist band where the zip falls short of the top edge.

Finally you need to finish the bottom edge of your skirt.

You can hem the edge, or you can use bias binding to finish it and to add decoration (see p. 42 overleaf). Hemming simply means folding an edge up, so that a raw edge is replaced with a neat folded edge.

Before making your hem, try your skirt on to check that you are happy with the length. If it is too long, put a pin in at the point where you would like your skirt to hang (indicated with a yellow pin on the first diagram above). Take the skirt off and insert a second pin, 1cm below your first. (Indicated by a red pin in the diagram). Trim off any excess fabric horizontally at the level of this pin.

Zig-zag stitch the raw edge all the way round. Turn your skirt inside out so you are looking at the wrong side of the fabric. Fold 1cm of the edge up so that you can see an even strip of the right side of your fabric all the way around the bottom of your skirt. You need to sew it down with a line of straight stitch running about 5mm away from the edge.

You can pin the edge into place, or if you are confident you can sew freestyle, slowly, folding as you go, holding the fold in place with your hands and letting the sewing machine do the work.

You have made a skirt :)

You can finish your skirt with bias binding instead of a hem.

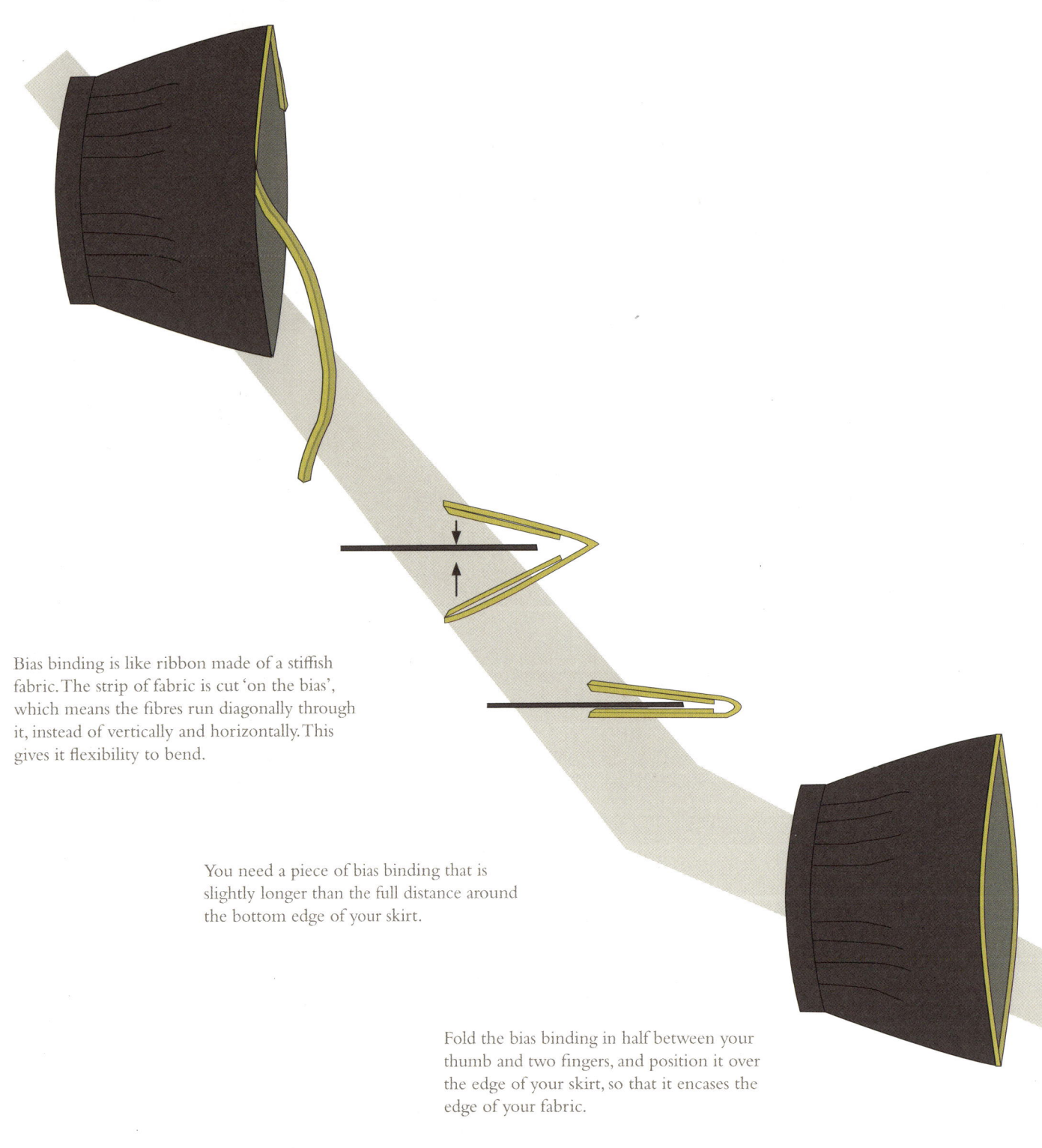

Bias binding is like ribbon made of a stiffish fabric. The strip of fabric is cut 'on the bias', which means the fibres run diagonally through it, instead of vertically and horizontally. This gives it flexibility to bend.

You need a piece of bias binding that is slightly longer than the full distance around the bottom edge of your skirt.

Fold the bias binding in half between your thumb and two fingers, and position it over the edge of your skirt, so that it encases the edge of your fabric.

Sew it down with straight stitch, catching both the front and back of your bias binding, with your fabric sandwiched in between.

You can make each side of your skirt from two (or more) pieces of fabric.

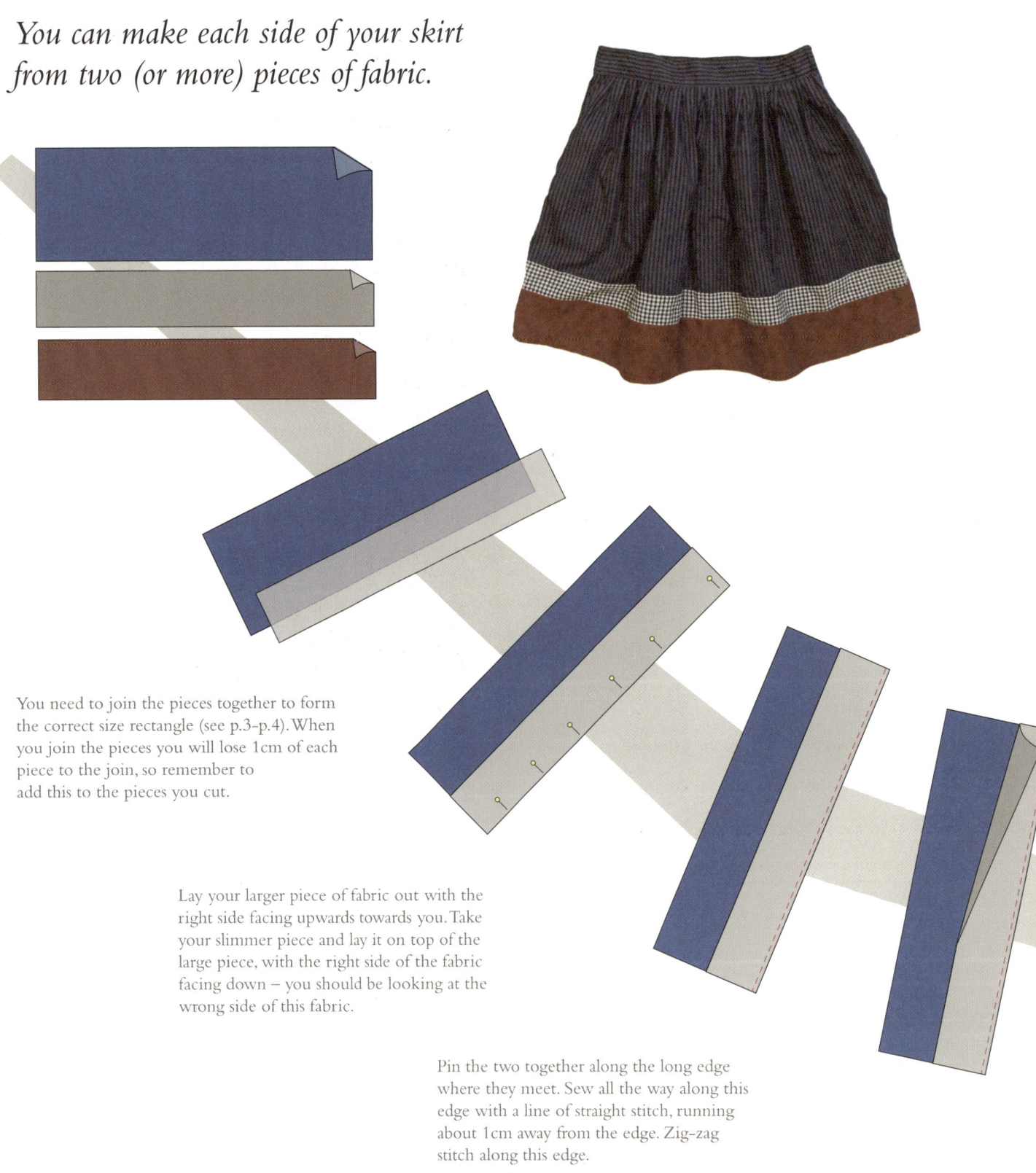

You need to join the pieces together to form the correct size rectangle (see p.3-p.4). When you join the pieces you will lose 1cm of each piece to the join, so remember to add this to the pieces you cut.

Lay your larger piece of fabric out with the right side facing upwards towards you. Take your slimmer piece and lay it on top of the large piece, with the right side of the fabric facing down – you should be looking at the wrong side of this fabric.

Pin the two together along the long edge where they meet. Sew all the way along this edge with a line of straight stitch, running about 1cm away from the edge. Zig-zag stitch along this edge.

Fold the slim strip of fabric downwards so that you are looking at the right sides of both pieces of fabric.

To flatten the two, run an iron over the join, or sew a line of straight stitch about 2mm away from the join, catching the flap of fabric at the back underneath as you sew.

SILKY BABIES

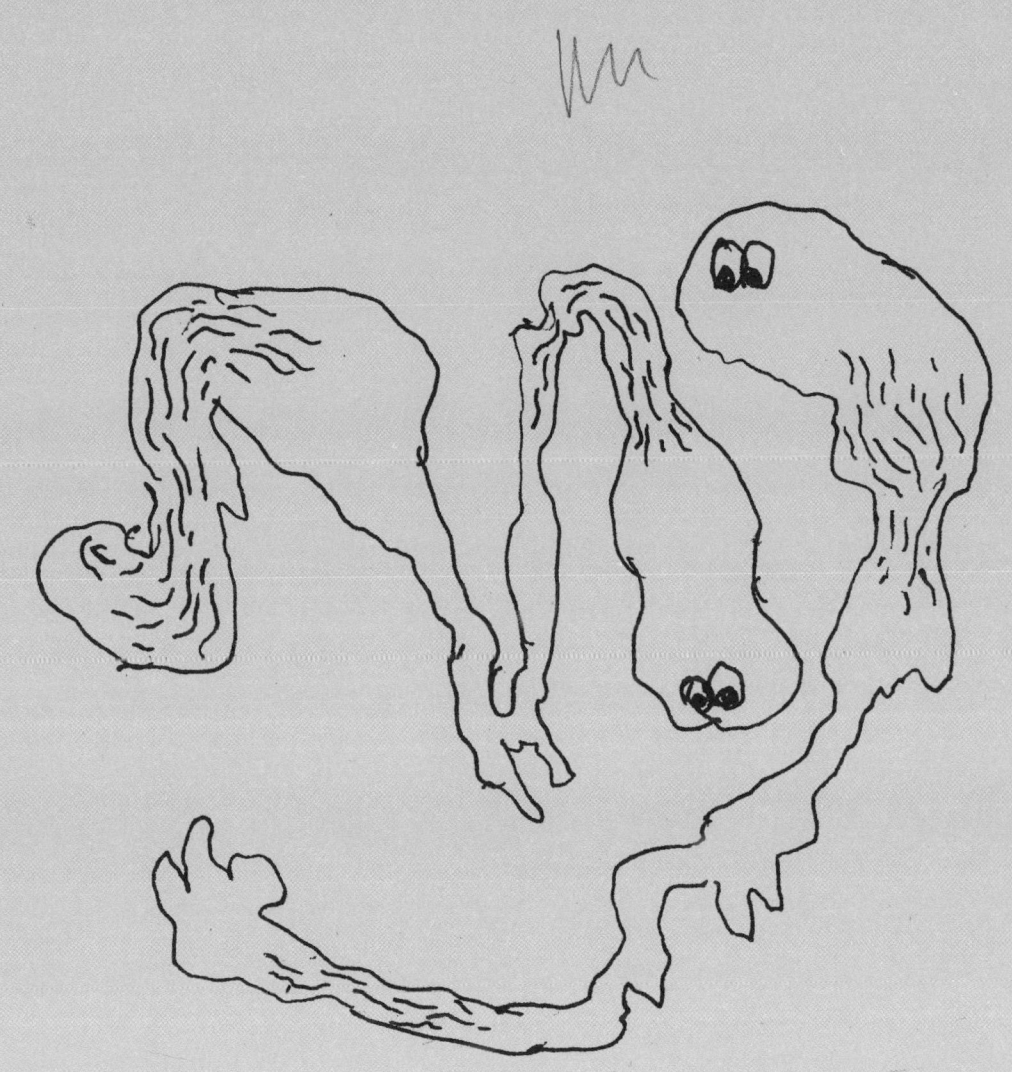

antuong nguyen

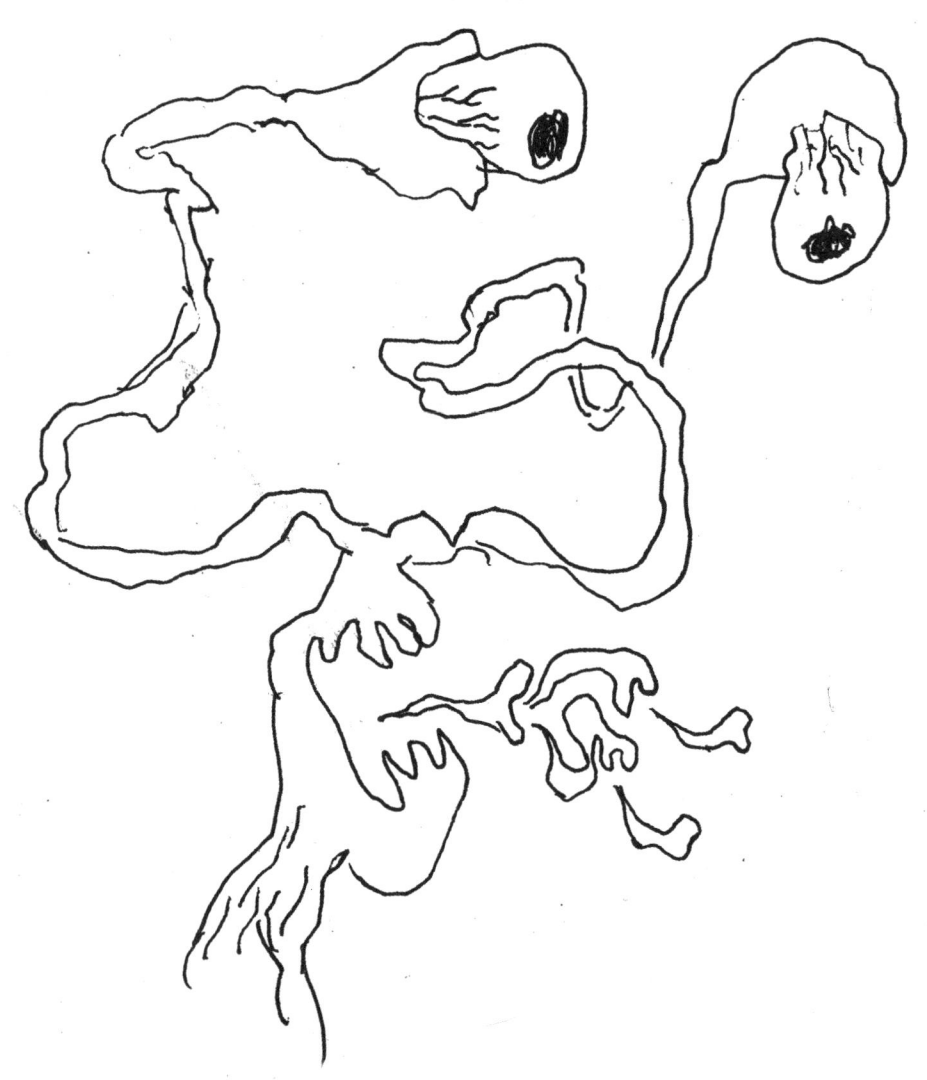

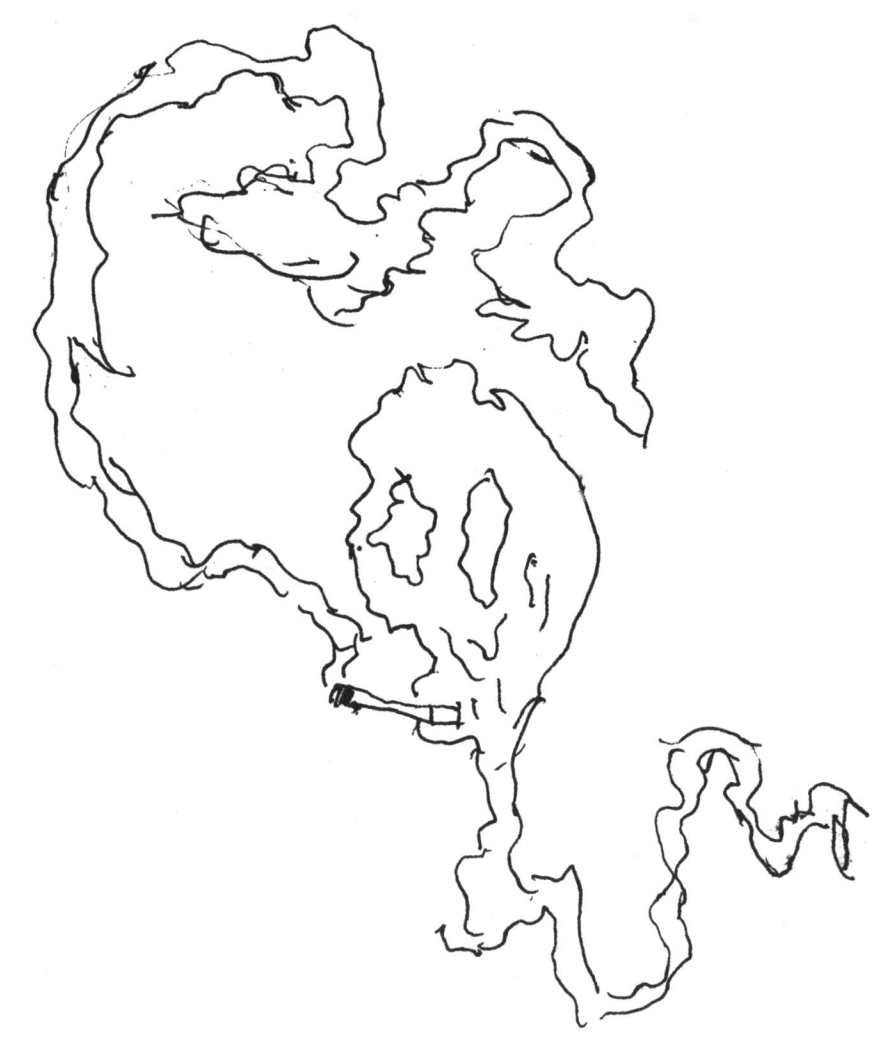

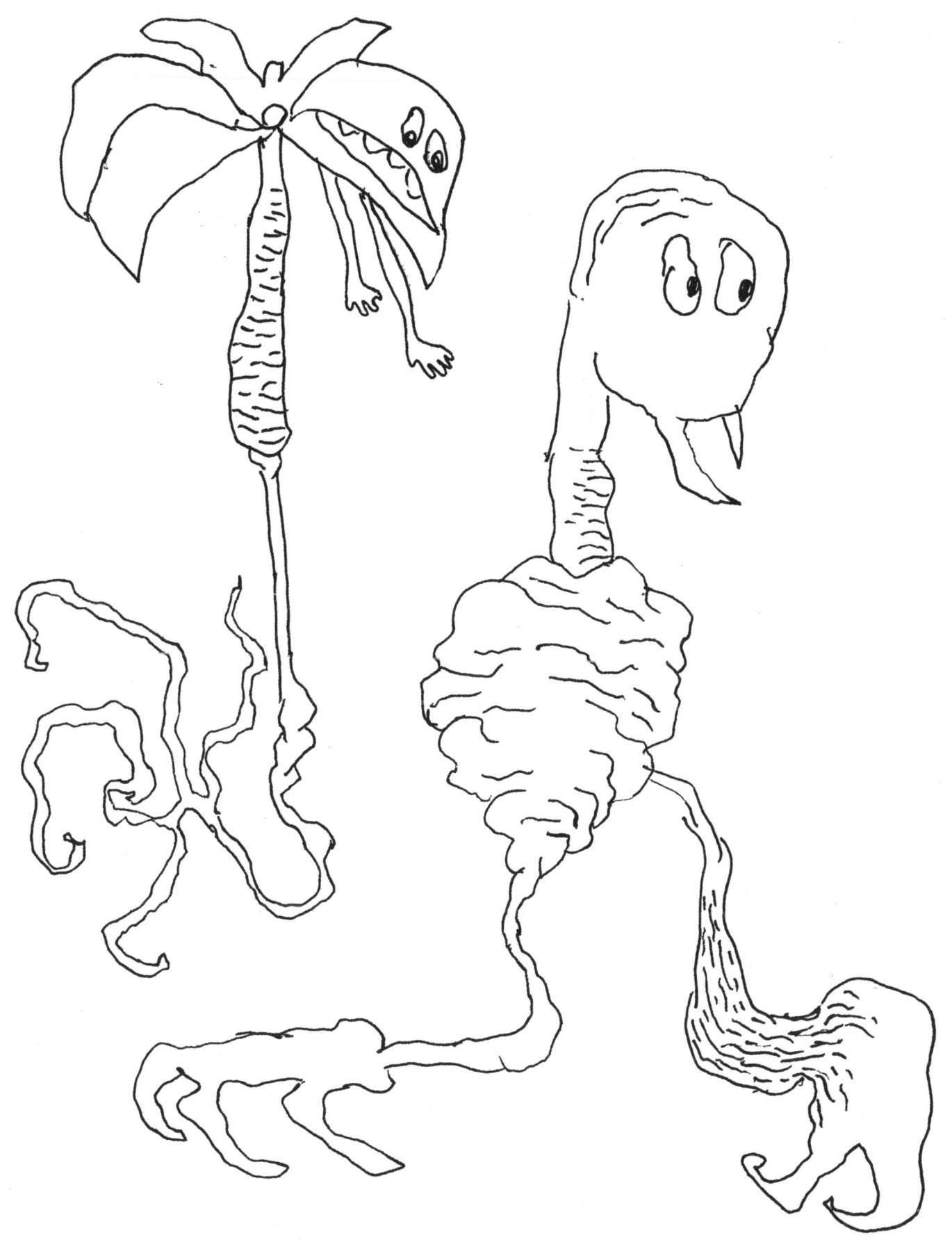